DESCARTES

A BEGINNER'S GUIDE

KEVIN O'DONNELL

Hodder & Stoughton

A MEMBER OF THE HODDER HEADLINE GROUP

Orders: please contact Bookpoint Ltd, 130 Milton Park, Abingdon, Oxon OX14 4SB. Telephone: (44) 01235 827720, Fax: (44) 01235 400454. Lines are open from 9.00–6.00, Monday to Saturday, with a 24-hour message answering service. Email address: orders@bookpoint.co.uk

British Library Cataloguing in Publication Data
A catalogue record for this title is available from The British Library

ISBN 0 340 84501 5

First published 2001
Impression number   10 9 8 7 6 5 4 3 2 1
Year   2007 2006 2005 2004 2003 2002 2001

Copyright © 2001 Kevin O'Donnell

All rights reserved. No part of this publication may be reproduced or transmitted in any form or by any means, electronic or mechanical, including photocopy, recording, or any information storage and retrieval system, without permission in writing from the publisher or under licence from the Copyright Licensing Agency Limited. Further details of such licences (for reprographic reproduction) may be obtained from the Copyright Licensing Agency Limited, of 90 Tottenham Court Road, London, W1P 9HE.

Cover photo from Bettmann/Corbis
Cover illustration by Jacey

Typeset by Transet Limited, Coventry, England.
Printed in Great Britain for Hodder & Stoughton Educational, a division of Hodder Headline Plc, 338 Euston Road, London NW1 3BH by Cox & Wyman, Reading, Berks

CONTENTS

CHAPTER 1: THE FIRST MODERN PHILOSOPHER	1
What is philosophy?	1
The Schoolmen	1
Descartes – the first modern philosopher?	3
Summary	5

CHAPTER 2: RENÉ DESCARTES: A LIFE	6
Give me the child…	6
Army days	7
The stove-heated room	8
Dreams and visions	8
The wanderer	8
Settled in Holland	10
The end of his life	11
In conclusion	11
Summary	12

CHAPTER 3: THE SCIENTIST	13
Algebra and geometry	13
The world	14
Light and vision	15
Meteors	16
Mistakes	17
Summary	18

CHAPTER 4: METHODS AND PRINCIPLES	19
Reductionism	19
Quantities and thinking things	20
Clear and distinct ideas	20

Prior and final causes	21
Observation and the scientific method	22
The Rationalist	23
Summary	24

CHAPTER 5: THE SCEPTIC AND THE COGITO — 25
A demonstration of some truths of Christianity?	25
The Meditations	25
The six days of meditations	26
Responses to *The Meditations*	30
Summary	32

CHAPTER 6: GOD — 33
Proving that God exists	33
The Cartesian circle	34
Causal adequacy	35
What can we make of the ontological argument?	36
Ultimate reality, or depth?	37
The God of philosophers	38
God and motion	39
Contact theory	41
So what did Descartes believe?	43
Summary	45

CHAPTER 7: THE SOUL — 46
Ghost in the machine?	47
Primitive notion	49
Sensing and representing	50
The Passions of the Soul	51
Can the mind affect the physical?	51
Can bodies affect the mind?	53

End thoughts	53
Summary	55

CHAPTER 8: BEAST-MACHINES: DESCARTES AND ANIMALS — 56

Animals as automata?	56
The bête-machine	56
Mere automata?	57
Not thinking and speaking	58
Conscious, but not self-so	59
And today?	59
Summary	60

CHAPTER 9: DESCARTES AND FEMINISM — 61

New insights	61
The mind–body split	62
Visualization	63
Nature and culture	66
Wonder and space	66
Decentring the self	68
Madness and reason	69
Ode to wholeness	70
Summary	71

CHAPTER 10: GOODBYE TO DESCARTES? — 72

Is the mind distinct from the body?	72
Can the universe be rationally examined?	79
In memoriam	84
Summary	85

GLOSSARY	86
FURTHER READING	88
INDEX	90

The First Modern Philosopher

WHAT IS PHILOSOPHY?

Philosophy is about clear thinking, and means, literally, 'love of wisdom'. Philosophers are concerned with the whole of knowledge and the whole of life. Traditionally, they have been concerned with the most fundamental truths about reality (the technical term for this is **metaphysics**). They have also thought about ethics, truth and justice. What surprises some is that they have often concerned themselves in the past with subjects that we would call mathematics or general science. The philosophers were also the early scientists, thinking clearly about life and the world around them. Science had not yet been born as a separate and value-neutral subject.

> **KEYWORD**
> Metaphysics: the examination of general features of reality beyond those described by natural science. The question of Meaning, of Being and of the foundations of truth.

THE SCHOOLMEN

The culture of Western Europe was largely held together by the Church in the Dark Ages and the Middle Ages. Learned clerics and monks absorbed Greek philosophy and saw this as a rational foundation upon which to build, only correcting it when it seemed to contradict the teaching of Scripture. Aristotle (384–322 BCE) was the Great Doctor, and his views were the foundation of Scholastic thought. The Scholastics, or the Schoolmen, followed Aristotle and others in setting out a compendium of knowledge that saw itself as total and final, or as much as human beings could grasp with their reason. This process was begun by learned pagan converts in late Roman times, such as St Augustine of Hippo (354–430), but the most influential of the Schoolmen was St Thomas Aquinas (1225–74). This Dominican friar and theologian wrote copiously and fixed Aristotelian concepts into Church life like cement. If God had given us the gift of reason, then genuine reason could not go against the tenets of the faith; if it did, then faith came first. Many of Aristotle's explanations of why things work the way they do are not explanations in the modern sense. Objects fall because they have a built-in propensity to do so, for example, or a magnet has a propensity to attract iron. But why? The Schoolmen would reply, 'Because that is how God made them'.

All that could be revealed to human reason had been revealed – it was a closed system. New ideas had to be sneaky. They had to claim that they were implied in earlier texts, so that commentaries on old works became a suitable cover for new ideas. The problem was that with a powerful (and often corrupt) Church, freethinkers could find themselves in trouble with groups such as the Inquisition. Some were daring to think more freely, and science was being born as a discipline with a method of observation and experimentation. People were prepared to go out and look at things rather than rely on old texts. The sixteenth and seventeenth centuries were to be a time of challenge, with the shaking of established thought and authority.

KEY FACT

Rebirth of Learning and Enlightenment

Trade routes and explorers opened up the Near East to the Western European states at the end of the first millennium. The Muslims had preserved texts from classical Greece which had been lost in the West. Muslim scholars translated these into Arabic and their civilization was ahead of the West in some matters of technology and medicine as a result. These texts were brought back to the monasteries where they were translated. The ancient wisdom led to a rebirth of learning (the 'Renaissance') in the early centuries of the second millennium. This was particularly true in the city states of Italy with their wealthy and active merchant class. It was still a pre-scientific age in some ways, though, for alchemy and superstition were mixed in with observation of the natural world. It was in this arena that the Schoolmen flourished and reigned supreme, guarded by the authority of the Church. The seventeenth century saw the rise of new, more scientific and rational philosophy which birthed the scientific method and began a period of new learning and invention known as the Enlightenment, or the Age of Reason.

DESCARTES – THE FIRST MODERN PHILOSOPHER?

René Descartes (1596–1650) lived during the later period of the Schoolmen and at the start of the Enlightenment. He made a significant and lasting contribution to the history of philosophy and the rise of the scientific method. When he was a young man, new inventions in lens-making and telescopes had started to revolutionize how people viewed the heavens. Galileo (1564–1642) was a contemporary, and his observations confirmed the earlier views of Copernicus, who in 1543, was the first to suggest that the earth orbited around the sun. Kepler confirmed Copernicus' ideas by mathematics in 1590. Galileo went a step further by testing the calculations by actual observation.

New ideas came from actually looking through a telescope and drawing your own conclusions. Aristotle had argued that the planets were perfect spheres, not marked by any incorruption. He thought the earth was at the centre and not the sun. Telescopes revealed a different story, and the planets, for example, were pot-marked and craggy. Descartes had been working on ideas that placed the sun at the centre since 1629, but upon hearing about Galileo's difficulties with the Church in Italy, he quietly shut up and stopped the planned publication of his work on the subject. Galileo found some in the Church to be initially supportive, but these ideas were seen ultimately as contradicting the Scriptures, and Galileo was placed under house arrest in 1633 and agreed not to publicize his views any further.

KEY FACT

Galileo's Wisdom

Nature is as divine a text as the holy Scriptures. They can't be in real contradiction with each other ...

The Bible teaches us how to go to heaven, not how the heavens go.

(from *The Two Great Systems of the World*)

Descartes was to pursue various studies and theories of science, some of which soon dated and have fallen away. At a time of an immense **paradigm shift** in thought, he set out the rational foundations of the scientific method, applying philosophical principles to the discoveries and observations that he and others were making. He provided a sure conceptual footing for science to develop.

Descartes' lasting fame lies in forming fundamental philosophical axioms that broke away from the traditions of the past, and looked critically for themselves at life. He pursued a rigorous scepticism, testing and seeking a sure point for knowledge. What our reason, our minds, ourselves, make of things, is important, not just what ancient thinkers had to say. He swept the decks clean, and for this reason he is known as the father of modern philosophy. After him, philosophers could again be more honest and enquiring. Descartes' lasting contribution, then, was in the field of **epistemology**. The system or science of knowledge itself concerned him, and his observations confirmed this, conducted according to strict rules of experimentation.

> **KEYWORDS**
>
> Paradigm shift: a shift in the perception we have of something and the models we use to understand it. Thomas Kuhn (b. 1922) coined the term, arguing that our knowledge did not generally grow like a slow escalator, but it came in flashes of inspiration, in leaps and as a result of new discoveries that render previous paradigms obsolete. Sometimes there is suspicion and conflict as the old order gives way. Descartes and the early Rationalists found exactly this in the reactions of the Church and the Schoolmen.
>
> Epistemology: the nature of knowledge, its sources and methods of learning.

✳ ✳ ✳ SUMMARY ✳ ✳ ✳

- Philosophy means 'love of wisdom' and is about clear thinking. Philosophers are interested in metaphysics, ethics, politics and linguistics. Before science was born as a separate discipline in itself, philosophers were also interested in scientific theories.

- The Schoolmen, or the Scholastics, were Christian theologians who adapted the Greek philosophers, Aristotle especially, to fit in with Scripture and Church teaching. The greatest Schoolman was Thomas Aquinas. It was believed that no new knowledge was possible outside of this system of philosophy.

- Descartes can be called the first modern philosopher because he introduced the fundamental principles of the scientific method, based upon reason and observation. He employed a healthily sceptical method, questioning all earlier foundations and presuppositions.

2 René Descartes: A Life

Descartes was a solider and a wanderer before he became established as a philosopher. He was a gentleman volunteer, an officer cadet, in the service of the Dutch prince of Nassau. He avoided combat at all costs, and treated his army time as a means of travelling and of attending a glorified military academy for young noblemen on the continent. In fact, he did as little work as possible, and when, in 1622 aged 26, he sold several properties given to him by his father, he was a wealthy man who never needed to work again.

The military service he found himself in was often undisciplined and inactive. The closest he ever seems to have been to any fighting was on a boat trip. He was on board ship with his valet when he heard the sailors conspiring to kill him and steal his money. He unsheathed his sword and threatened to run them through in a swaggering and desperate show of bravery. They backed down and took him to his destination.

His delicacy of frame and his idleness meant that he spent 12 hours a day in bed, never rising before 11.00 a.m. if he could help it! And yet, this man is remembered as one of the great philosophers and the first modern philosopher.

GIVE ME THE CHILD ...

Descartes was born on 31 March 1596, in Touraine in northern France. His grandfather was a doctor and his father was a lawyer and local magistrate. On his mother's side of the family, there was a long line of legal officials. Descartes was probably part of the minor aristocracy, brought up in an affluent and well-educated family.

His interest in science and deeper philosophical issues began with his training at La Flèche, the Jesuit college in Anjou. Descartes was sent there when he was ten and stayed for eight years. During his last two years there he taught mathematics and physics. He excelled at mathematics and this was the one thing he later claimed to have gained from his education. Physics was not the physics that we know now; it was **Scholasticism** using the old properties of Aristotle. The Jesuits were progressive, though, celebrating the discovery of the moons of Jupiter by the enormously suspect Galileo. They might, also, have provided the young Descartes and other students with new optical instruments for studying the stars. These were on sale in Paris as early as 1609.

> **KEYWORD**
>
> Scholasticism: the general term for the schools of philosophy that dominated European universities prior to the time of Descartes. The idea of the Greek philosophers, especially Aristotle, interpreted in a Christian context, were central to this philosophy, which formed the basis of medieval intellectual life.

After leaving La Flèche, Descartes took a law degree at Poitiers in 1616, as his older brother Pierre had done some years earlier. Still, his father seems to have decided that law would not be the young René's career, and he was sent to join the army at Breda in Holland in 1618 as a gentleman volunteer for Prince Maurice of Nassau.

ARMY DAYS

At Breda, when he was 22, Descartes met a doctor older than him, Isaac Beeckman. They started a lasting friendship and corresponded for some years. Descartes claimed that Beeckman had shocked him out of his idleness and had started him thinking again. The deep discussions and disputations were mathematical, and Descartes said that he had once solved four long-standing mathematical problems in six days, and that he wanted to give the public a new science whereby any mathematical or geometrical problem could be solved. He was seeking basic, clear principles with which to analyse knowledge.

THE STOVE-HEATED ROOM

Descartes travelled in a circuitous route to avoid troop movements via Amsterdam, Poland, Bohemia and Frankfurt. Descartes reached Frankfurt in time to witness the coronation of the Emperor Ferdinand.

In the cold month of November, Descartes found himself shivering in the Bavarian winter and he withdrew into a stove-heated room on 10 November 1619. This was to be a turning point, for he had a vision in the daytime and a series of three dreams which he felt were outlining the course of his life.

DREAMS AND VISIONS

The details of the daytime vision are not clear, but the three dreams are described as follows:

> I was jostled by a whirlwind which tried to push me over.
>
> I ran for shelter in a college. I met an old friend who gave me a melon to eat from a distant land.
>
> I was in bed looking at a pile of books. There was an encyclopaedia and an anthology of poems.

Descartes had been terrified by the first two dreams, and he thought a demon was attacking him. The third dream was calming, and gave him the direction he was looking for. After the turbulence and confusion, he was to find a sure path in the study of knowledge. He was to abandon a career in the military for a life of learning.

THE WANDERER

To use Descartes' own words, he did nothing after his vision 'but roam about in the world'. He wanted to expose himself to different customs and attitudes to free himself of the in-built prejudices of his upbringing so that he could think all the more clearly. He resumed military service for a brief spell in 1621, in Silesia and Poland. He was back in France in 1622, and a letter dated May of that year delivered the news that a number of properties which his father had given him had been sold. He now had the necessary wealth never to have to work for a living again. His strong religious feelings are revealed in his pilgrimage to Our Lady of Loretto in Italy, where he gave thanks for his visions. He returned to France in 1625, and nearly bought the lieutenant-generalship of Chatellerault, but it was far too costly.

He settled in Paris from 1626 to 1628 and this gave him the time and companionship for his ideas to develop. He was in the company of intellectuals who stimulated debate, and he befriended Marin Mersenne, a Minim friar who had known Descartes at La Flèche. Mersenne kept Descartes abreast of new developments, and Descartes defended his mentor and friend when he attacked the atheistic **libertines** of the period. Descartes defended the doctrine of God and the soul, and Mersenne was influenced by Descartes' developing belief in the reliability of mathematics for the basis of a sound science. Anti-Scholastic feeling was stirring, and in 1624, a public meeting in Paris to hear a criticism of Aristotle was banned by the Sorbonne.

> **KEYWORD**
> Libertines: atheistic free-thinkers who rejected Scholasticism and the teachings of the Church.

The rejection of Aristotle created something of a vacuum for the study of the natural sciences. There were those who felt that science – a body of stable, consistent, observations and rules about life – was impossible as such things were far beyond human minds. Certain that mathematics could provide the groundwork of all knowledge, Descartes was on a quest for a theory of everything.

Also, at this time, Descartes befriended Jean Ferrier, a Parisian lens and instrument maker. This was another passion, to study the heavens and the science of lenses and light, mapping in so closely to his love of mathematics.

SETTLED IN HOLLAND

Decartes moved to Holland in 1628. He wanted more solitude to reflect and to study. Holland was also a more libertine environment where freethinkers might flourish. He tried to get Ferrier to come with him and to patent a machine for making telescopic lenses. Ferrier would not budge, and this was a huge lost opportunity, for such a device, produced so early by two great minds, would have made their respective names in a different sphere.

Descartes had a daughter, Francine, by his servant girl, Hélène, in Amsterdam. Sadly, she died aged five from scarlet fever. He was devastated and never fully recovered. He kept his address secret during this time. He often had all his mail sent to Mersenne's house who passed it on. (Mersenne acted as Descartes' publicist and advocate from the late 1620s.) One traveller did find out where he was; de Sorbière journeyed around Europe seeking out conversations with the intellectuals of the day. He found Descartes in a small chateau about two hours from the sea, with servants and gardens with an orchard beyond. De Sorbière was received courteously and politely.

The middle-aged Descartes developed eccentricities. He wore wigs made for him in Paris – he had four when he died. He dressed neatly and usually in black, wearing a sword when he journeyed any distance. He ate little meat, preferring berries and roots and adored omelettes made from eggs that were ten days old!

The idler in him lived on as he never rose before 11.00 a.m., writing and thinking in bed. Yet, he took regular exercise, too, and regarded his body as a well-built machine that needed maintenance.

He could be overwhelmingly generous to strangers and to servants, such as the shoemaker Rembrantsz whom he instructed in philosophy and astronomy.

During this time, he toyed with the formation of a universal language, adapted from Latin. He did not get very far. He did, however, publish his great works during his years in Holland: *Discourse on the Method* (1637), *Meditations* (1641) and *Principles of Philosophy* (1644). These set out his doubts and methods in establishing sound philosophical discourse. Other works included *Geometry, Dioptrics* and *Meteors* known as *The Essays* (1637), presenting his key scientific ideas, and *Passions of the Soul* (1649) outlining the bases of ethics and psychology.

THE END OF HIS LIFE

In retirement, Descartes pottered about in his garden, growing vegetables, and he supervised translations of his works into French from their original Latin. Latin was still widely used as the intellectual language of the day. He withdrew more and more from contemporary debates and devoted his final thoughts to ethical questions. It seems that he visited England in 1640, and it is rumoured that he returned in 1641, but he certainly seemed to have no intentions of moving there. He corresponded with Queen Christina of Sweden for several years before she invited him to be her philosophy tutor. She was unconventional in dress and manner, being fiercely intellectual. She spoke six languages. The problem was that the busy monarch wished to begin her tutorials at 5.00 a.m.! Descartes had to abandon the late-rising traditions of a lifetime and get up in the cold and the dark in a land of 'bears, rocks and ice' as he put it.

This broke him. In 1650 he died of pneumonia. In 1663 the Roman Catholic Church banned his books and placed them on the **Index of Forbidden Books**.

IN CONCLUSION

Descartes was the first modern philosopher, standing as a hinge between the ancient world and the modern. He flung aside the teachings of Aristotle and opened up interest in mathematics, regular laws and natural

KEYWORD

Index of Forbidden Books: a list of prohibited literature whose teachings were said to contradict the Church's faith and morals. This was instituted in 1557 and lasted until 1917! Special permission had to be sought to read anything on this list.

observation. Yet, he had a mystical side. His visions started his dedication to philosophy, and he was a committed **theist** and a believer in the immortal soul.

> **KEYWORD**
>
> Theist: a believer in God, the Supreme Being.

---

* * *SUMMARY* * *

- Descartes was born in 1596 in northern France. His family were doctors and magistrates.

- He was educated at the progressive Jesuit college of La Flèche for eight years. He developed a love of mathematics and taught physics. He might have used new optical instruments whilst here.

- He took a law degree in 1616 and then entered military service. He struck up a friendship with Isaac Beeckman who started him thinking again, puzzling over mathematical problems.

- He had a vision and three dreams in a stove-heated room which convinced him to devote his life to learning and philosophy. He wandered around Europe for several years seeking new ideas and experience.

- He settled in Paris for two years and became a lifelong friend of the friar Marin Mersenne, who was to become his apologist.

- A move to Holland came in 1628 where he stayed until near the end of his life. Holland was a more open and tolerant society for freethinkers. It was here that he wrote his major works – *Discourse on Method*, *Meditations* and *Discourse on Philosophy*.

- Descartes died in 1650 after travelling to Sweden to teach Queen Christina. His 5.00 a.m. sessions and the cold brought the onset of pneumonia.

The Scientist 3

Descartes was a contemporary of leading scientific thinkers in the seventeenth century. Francis Bacon (1561–1626), for example, rose to prominence as Lord Chancellor in Britain, writing his *Advancement of Learning* in 1605 and *Novum Organum* in 1620. He encouraged the inductive method as taught by Aristotle. We observe natural events and objects and learn from them, rather than deducing ideas about them from within our own reason. Aristotle laid the foundations of the future scientific method by teaching people to generalize from particulars. If we see an animal with webbed feet that can swim, then all animals with webbed feet can swim, or so we should be able to assume safely.

Galileo Galilei improved the refracting telescope while being professor of mathematics at Padua university in Italy and advanced radical cosmological theories, whereby the sun was at the centre of our solar system, and not the earth.

Descartes was maturing in an intellectual arena where principles, methods and mathematics, as well as careful observation, were the new foundations of knowledge rather than the authority of past tradition as taught by the Schoolmen, or Scholastics.

Mathematics and astronomy were the two fields that captivated the interest and genius of the young Descartes whilst at the Jesuit college of La Flèche.

ALGEBRA AND GEOMETRY
Descartes made a lasting contribution to the study of mathematics by refining the use of algebra. He had complained that existing forms of algebra and geometry needed to be streamlined to make them clearer

and easier to work with. Geometry was bound up with the examination of figures so that you could not think 'without greatly tiring the imagination'. Algebra was 'so confined to certain rules and symbols' that this resulted in a 'confused and obscure art'. Descartes introduced the convention of using x, y and z for unknown quantites, and knowns by a, b and c. He worked out the standard systems for cubes and roots of numbers, and turned to geometry to represent numerical relations in lines, and these, in turn, could be represented algebraically.

He wanted to use this simpler, clearer mathematical thinking for the solution of problems, and his *Regulae ad Directionem Ingenii* (Rules for the Direction of the Mind), written around 1628 but never completed, sought to apply these principles. About 21 of the rules are from his hand, and they seek to find a method to observe, rather than mere curiousity. He also tries to break problems down into their component or simpler parts, tackling each section at a time. We must go back and back further to the causes, and when you find something that is a cause and needs no further explanation, then this is an *absolute category*.

He turned his attention to the problem of the **anaclastic**. This is the optical problem whereby two parallel lines of light pass through a denser medium and intersect at some point. It was a conundrum; it should not have happened. He split this into its components and saw how the ratio of the angles actually is seen to vary as light passes through media of varying density.

THE WORLD

Descartes worked upon a treatise that sought a unified explanation for all natural phenomena. The sciences of his day were separate disciplines such as optics and mechanics, and the main four, the **quadrivium**, were arithmetic, geometry, music and astronomy. He sought a unified theory early on, and this was probably the weighty matter that beset

> **KEYWORDS**
>
> Anaclastic: parallel lines intersect when passing through a fluid as a result of a change in the angles of reflected light.
>
> Quadrivium: the academic study of arithmetic, geometry, music and astronomy as the main four sciences of the early seventeenth century.

him in the winter of 1619, and he mentioned this quest when writing to his friend Beeckman.

He had dabbled with Rosicrucianism in his youth, seeking any clues in their esoteric knowledge for a **unified theory** of the sciences. This was abandoned, but by the time he was working on *The World* in 1630, only published after his death, he had found the solution. Mathematics alone can form a unified understanding of different phenomena at a micro-level. *The World* was ready for press in 1633, but then came the news that Galileo had been condemned by the Inquisition for teaching that the earth revolved around the sun (as contained in his *Of the Two Great Systems of the World*). Descartes' own work had calculated that terrestial motion was more likely than the Scholastic model, and could not be excised from the book without damaging the rest. He did not go to print, fearing retribution. His ideas were revisited in his later *Essays*.

> **KEYWORD**
> Unified theory: a 'Theory of Everything' which seeks to find underlying forces or equations behind different physical forces and laws.

KEY FACT:
ROSICRUCIANS

Rosicrucianism began in the seventeenth century as a satirical jibe at first, in two German works by a Lutheran pastor. These claimed to tell the story of a traveller from the East who held many secrets of ancient wisdom, and an independent form of Christianity that was anti-catholic. This was mistaken as fact, and Rosicrucian groups and literature sprang up as a secret society. The Rose and the Cross are symbols of the resurrection and the Death of Christ.

LIGHT AND VISION

Descartes' *Dioptrics*, prepared by 1635 and finally published as part of his *Essays* in 1637, concerned itself with the refraction of light. He contrasted the appearance of light in different media, and of colours, with the movements of objects such as a ball bouncing off different surfaces. He intended to show how appearance was dependent upon contact between moving bodies. He explores the make-up of the human eye, how we perceive distance and the best types of lenses for long-range and microscopic viewing. He established lasting principles of refraction such as the sine law that describes how light is refracted according to the density of the medium it passes through. He made some errors, though, in assuming that the denser the medium, the quicker light would pass through it.

METEORS

This section of the *Essays* covered various topics in nature, such as terrestial bodies, salt, winds, clouds, rainbows and storms, to name but a few. He is concerned to explain particular phenomena by describing them as having many parts of motion, size, shape and arrangement of parts. Galileo had been working with similar notions. Descartes sought to strip away the scholastic insistence upon tracing properties of individual objects back to supposed forms and qualities which belong to different categories or classes of thing. Stones fell because that was their form or quality to do so, seeds to grow, the earth to turn. This explained nothing and invented an invisible *x* factor. Descartes used a 'single hypothesis' instead. The motion, shape, measurements and arrangements of matter alone can produce different results, for example, turning a solid into a liquid form. No further explanations are required. As Descartes remarked: 'Compare all their real qualities, their substantial forms, their elements and their other countless hypotheses with my single hypothesis that all bodies are composed of parts …'

There was still the question of how God was involved with this motion, whether directly or indirectly through the impact of secondary causes. There was also lively debate about whether the soul/mind, as well as God, could cause motion. Whatever people made of these more abstract ideas, Descartes' physical explanations of motion could not be bettered for their time. Recent theories have suggested that the understanding of motion lay behind much of the seventeenth century drive to observe the world, especially in the case of Galileo.

MISTAKES

Descartes had hit upon some important principles, and his contribution to knowledge about the laws of refraction was invaluable, as was his study of the nature of the rainbow, showing why it was a circular arc. He made some huge errors of calculation and of speculation, though. For example, the 'fact' that water freezes more quickly if it has been boiled first is nonsense. He also believed that all matter was made up of tiny 'corpuscles' that were endlessly divisible, and that matter existed by being extended out in the quantities of length, breadth and height. This made it impossible for a vacuum to exist. He also disputed the existence of atoms, as he feared that there was no material thing that was indivisible – only mental and spiritual states were. This is a 'fact' which has been opened up again since the advent of quantum physics as atoms break down into smaller components and the sub-atomic level seems to scramble all conventional logic. Is there ever a 'full stop' to matter at its lowest levels?

Descartes did not work with a theory of gravity, and so his universe was made up of swirling whirlpools of matter that interacted by direct contact with each other. Isaac Newton (1642–1727) demolished this theory and his ideas carried the day.

Descartes' thinking about the corpuscles broke them down into primary and secondary qualities. The primary qualities were the predictable, measurable, reliable properties that were accessible to mathematics and reason. The secondary qualities (like colour) were formed when the corpuscles acted upon our senses. These were a rough guide to reality and not necessarily what was actually out there. This was a vital distinction for Descartes, and his scepticism about our ability to really know anything tested the foundations of his epistemology and laid sure foundations for the rise of the scientific method. Unlike Bacon and Galileo, he had moved beyond the inductive method of observation and he sought deductive principles upon which to base future science. This was his original contribution and vision.

✷ ✷ ✷ SUMMARY ✷ ✷ ✷

- Descartes, along with Bacon and Galileo, worked from observation of the world rather than received wisdom. Descartes was to develop a procedure which bequeathed us with the scientific method.

- Early influences at La Flèche were in the fields of mathematics and optics.

- Descartes worked to make the practice of mathematics clearer, and reformed the rules of algebra. A key feature of his method was to break down problems into their smaller, component parts.

- Descartes tackled and solved the anaclastic problem, whereby parallel lines intersect when passing through fluids.

- Interest in forming a unified theory of knowledge led Descartes to become interested in the esoteric speculations of the Rosicrucians for a time. He eventually sought the answer in mathematics.

- Descartes worked with light, colours and reflection. He studied the human eye.

- His study of celestial bodies and their motion led him to formulate the concept of extended reality, whereby physical objects were to be understood as being made up of many parts and measurements. What exactly caused motion remained a difficulty.

- Descartes made many mistakes and followed false assumptions – water does not freeze quicker if has been boiled first, and the world is not made up of millions of corpuscles whirling around.

Methods and Principles

Descartes did not make a lasting contribution to actual or practical science. Other theories superseded his. His legacy is in the philosophy of science that helped to prepare the scientific method. The terms 'science' and 'philosophy' were not exact categories as they are now. They were interchangeable terms connoting knowledge. Descartes was working towards a synthesis of knowledge, a means of seeking an underlying unity between different aspects of 'science' (e.g. medicine, astronomy and physics) and between different physical objects. He often compared scientific knowledge to a tree, with metaphysics – the underlying method – as the roots, physics as the trunk, and the other fields such as astronomy and geometry as the branches. His unifying theory was found in mathematics Here we were dealing with measurable and predictable elements that applied to all forms of knowledge about the physical world. This moved beyond the authority of the Scholastics with their closed system of knowledge based upon the Bible and Aristotle.

REDUCTIONISM

Descartes was a **reductionist** in so far as he believed that physical objects could be broken down and analysed in terms of their constituent parts.

> In this volume I have deduced the causes – which I believe to be quite evident – of these and many other phenomena from principles which are known to all and admitted by all, namely the shape, size, position and motion of particles of matter. And anyone who considers all this will

KEYWORD

Reductionist: analysing the external world as reducible to the sum of its parts, to basic, physical properties. Today the term tends to imply that a thinker denies the existence of an immaterial, immortal soul or the spiritual realm. This was not true for Descartes and many seventeenth-century reductionists. A distinction was drawn between the mental/spiritual and the physical.

readily be convinced that there are no powers in stones and plants that are so mysterious, and no marvels attributed to 'sympathetic' and 'antipathetic' influences that are so astonishing, that they cannot be explained in this way. In short there is nothing in the whole of nature, nothing, that is, which should be referred to purely corporeal causes, i.e. those devoid of thought, and mind, which is incapable of being deductively explained on the basis of these self-same principles...

(*Principles of Philosophy*, Part IV)

QUANTITIES AND THINKING THINGS

Descartes drew a sharp distinction, however, between the mind (or soul) and physical nature. He differentiated between *res extensa* and *res cogitans*, between *extended substance* and *thinking substance*. Physical realities were **extended realities**, as they had the dimensions of length, breadth and height, and were thus quantifiable. Intellectual properties were not explicable by measurement and the quantitive language of physics. Descartes is often called a dualist as he posits these two aspects to reality and to the individual human being. Why he said this, how separate he really thought them to be and the abiding questions this raises for philosophy will be considered later.

> **KEYWORD**
>
> Extended reality: that which is measurable and quantifiable. It has length, breadth and height, weight and motion.

Descartes arrived at this conclusion through his difficulty in establishing how real we might believe the external world to be. He mistrusted his sense experience as a reliable guide because our senses can mislead us (e.g. why should we think that the earth beneath us is moving?) and he sought underlying, eternal, universal truths in geometry and mathematics.

CLEAR AND DISTINCT IDEAS

Descartes spoke of 'clear and distinct ideas' that were deduced internally by the power of reason alone, and were not dependent upon sense experience. These included the rules of mathematics. He argued that a substance such as wax was so variable to the senses (hard if cold, soft if warm, smelling of honey or flowers and solid or liquid to the eyes) that we could have no reliable knowledge of it apart from the underlying mathematical properties that it possessed. By a clear idea, he did not only mean seeing numbers in the mind, and the logical steps in an equation, but concepts themselves. Such an idea is singular, indivisible and not confused with others, 'precisely distinguished from all others, so that it contains no element that is not clear'.

It might be objected that we could form an inner concept that is very clear to us, such as the moon being made of green cheese, but it is not actually real. Descartes combined his 'clear ideas' with mathematical measurement, and actual observation of objects, though. There was a dynamic that produced 'knowledge', but he believed that there was an innate faculty within each of us that perceived the true nature of things without the senses.

PRIOR AND FINAL CAUSES

The Schoolmen followed Aristotle in teaching that everything had a **final cause**. It was appointed a purpose in the world, such as a knife has the nature to cut. Fire, too, has the nature to move upwards, and heavy weights fall down. This is their function, their 'purpose', and everything is related to a final goal or purpose of the world. Causation was thus teleological, aiming at some 'end'.

> **KEYWORD**
> Final cause: the Schoolmen thought than an object was made with a purpose in mind by God, which was its final cause. So, fire burned, warmed and moved upwards because of its in-built, inner propensity to do so.

Descartes rejected the notion of final causes, arguing that the prior cause was what mattered. Their final cause or destiny was an occult mystery known only to God alone. The scientist was to investigate the causes prior to effects. Rather than an almost magical, animistic world, where things have ill-defined qualities that work on each other, things become more mechanistic and predictable.

OBSERVATION AND THE SCIENTIFIC METHOD

This investigation involved some level of observation and experimentation. Aristotle had argued that we must observe natural phenomena and classify different kinds of objects. It was logical to made inductive generalizations from particulars to universals, such as 'this dog barks, therefore all dogs can bark'. There is, of course, something provisional about statements like this. One day we might discover a dog that cannot bark, for whatever reason, and David Hume was to scold some empiricist philosophers for basing all their beliefs on what they could see and thus assuming that they had discovered immutable laws. Still, the scientific method works by such observation and tabulation, forming the best working hypothesis or explanation at any one given time (though with the advent of new knowledge this might be revised).

Descartes produced basic rules for scientific observation which he published in his *Discourse on the Method* in 1637. These are the main ideas:

* Trust only what is clear to the mind – i.e. what is deduced and indivisible.

* Split large problems into smaller units.

* Argue from the simple to the complex.

* Check over your results when finished.

Descartes also rejected the complicated Scholastic classification of things into all sorts of common-sense properties such as 'dryness' or 'heaviness' or 'sweetness'. Whereas they would have spoken of an apple that had the categories of red and sweetness, he spoke of a red, sweet apple. Beneath the psychological, or sense-experienced aspects of colour and taste, he saw objects perceived in this or that particular way.

THE RATIONALIST

For all the reductionism of Descartes, he was also a **Rationalist**. The Rationalists believed that the surest form of knowledge came from within the mind, from reason, and not observation. The Empiricists argued the latter. Descartes was returning more to Plato rather than to Aristotle. Plato stressed that reason gave us the truest truth, probing behind the changing world of forms to the realm of the Ideals. These were abstract and mathematical, of more abiding worth than the fleeting beauty of a sunset, for example 2 + 2 must always equal 4. Thus, to return to his thoughts on wax, he declared, 'I know the nature of this wax…purely by mental perception…'.

Descartes perhaps confused two forms of necessity, those of logic and cause. That 2 + 2 = 4 is a matter of logical necessity, but other things must have a *cause* for their behaviour which might not always be worked out by mathematics. We guess these based upon our past experience. This tension between empirical observation and inner intuition lies not only at the heart of Descartes' thought, but of subsequent philosophy and ideas of science.

> **KEYWORD**
>
> Rationalist: someone who believes that true knowledge comes from reason and is more reliable than that apprehended by the senses through contact and observation.

> **KEY FACT**
> **THE INDUCTIVE METHOD**
>
> This method is working out the action and behaviour of some-thing by observation. The deductive method works from principles and applies them to situations.

✳ ✳ ✳ SUMMARY ✳ ✳ ✳

- Descartes' legacy was more in the underlying philosophy and methodology of scientific investigation than in actual practical discoveries and inventions.

- The method which Descartes developed worked by reducing problems to their component parts, and arguing from the smallest aspect to the more complex.

- He separated the two realms of mind and material nature, the *rescogitans* and the *res extensa*.

- Rational intuition could discern 'clear and distinct' ideas about the nature of things that might vary to the naked eye or to the other senses, such as wax.

- Final causes were rejected, looking for other explanations in the motion and make-up of objects.

- The inductive method was followed but Descartes was also a Rationalist, seeking concepts and formulae intuitively and logically that were more sure than sensory data.

The Sceptic and The Cogito

A DEMONSTRATION OF SOME TRUTHS OF CHRISTIANITY?

Descartes began work on *The Meditations* in November 1639, having started to write down ideas on metaphysics in 1629. He now determined to write these up in a mature form that was publishable. He had been living in Holland for ten years by this time. As he wrote, he was facing more and more suspicion and criticism from the Jesuits and he was constantly concerned to clarify difficulties with them and to try to meet the objections of the theologians. He claimed that the work was a demonstration of some of the truths of Christianity, though, underneath, it was a systematic attempt to undermine the philosophy of Aristotle and the Scholastics. After writing the work, he approached two groups of theologians to make their corrections, both in Holland and at the Sorbonne. His friend and apologist Mersenne also set about collecting the opinions of other churchmen. Seven sets of *Objections* were written, and Descartes added his *Replies* to these, forming a large appendix to the 1641 edition.

THE MEDITATIONS

Descartes constructed his work in an unusual manner, following the format of reflective, spiritual exercises, such as those of St Ignatius. There were six meditations each of which took a day. These overturned the usual rules of analytic style, which proceeded from first premises onwards to the conclusion. Some of Descartes' earlier ideas were overthrown and rejected as erroneous as he reached the end of the work.

Descartes is determined to face all his doubts and to reject anything that cannot be seen as certain and, therefore, as a sure foundation for thought:

Several years have now elapsed since I first became aware that I had accepted, even from my youth, many false opinions for true, and that consequently what I afterwards based on such principles was highly doubtful; and from that time I was convinced of the necessity of undertaking once in my life to rid myself of all the opinions I had adopted, and of commencing anew the work of building from the foundation, if I desired to establish a firm and abiding superstructure in the sciences …

(Meditation I)

THE SIX DAYS OF MEDITATIONS
The six days considered the following themes:

Day one: Of the things of which we may doubt
Knowledge gained through the senses can be misleading; we might hallucinate, suffer the effects of an optical illusion or interpret data wrongly, for example. We might, in truth, be dreaming that we are awake, just as we can have very vivid dreams. Descartes imagines that the fire he is sitting by, and the pen and paper he holds in his hand, are just in his mind. Even then, these images would be based upon general realities and given things. Even fantastical paintings of satyrs make use of given objects and features of humans and animals. From these general objects we can deduce the principles of mathematics and other sciences. Surely these are steadfast and trustworthy?

Descartes then becomes rather playful, inventing the figure of a deceiving demon whose task it is to trick us constantly. All our senses and even the general principles of mathematics might be delusions.

Day two: Of the nature of the human mind; and that it is more easily known than the body
Descartes strips away all doubt with the realization that even if a demon does deceive us, then there is *someone* who is being deceived – the 'me' in my head. Descartes trusts his thoughts and the consciousness that has them:

> So it must, in fine, be maintained, all things being maturely and carefully considered that this proposition I am, I exist (*cogito, ergo sum*), is necessarily true each time it is expressed by me, or conceived in my mind.
>
> (Meditation II)

This is his famous dictum, **cogito, ergo sum**, often translated as 'I think, therefore I am'. This is the one attribute of the soul that is self-evident and existent, whereas others, such as perception, depend upon the body and the senses.

> **KEYWORD**
>
> Cogito, ergo sum: I think (or I am thinking) therefore I am.

Day three: Of God: that he exists

God is invoked to secure the truth of the cogito and of the deduced truth of general principles and objects. A good God, who is perfect, would not deceive us. We might be finite and capable of error, especially when we are careless and jump to conclusions, but the world is there, I am there, because God is.

His 'proof' of God in this section is based upon the idea of God having to represent a greater reality, namely God himself. He argues that if such an idea is in his finite mind, then an infinite deity must have placed it there. It could not have come from his own imagination alone: 'I should not, however, have the idea of an infinite substance, seeing I am a finite being, unless it were given me by some substance in reality finite.'

Day four: Of truth and error

Descartes expands upon the cogito and the nature of God, and of how the attributes of the cogito – knowledge, will and imagination – are pale reflections of the infinite attributes of God. He imagines that he is midway between the Being of God and Nothingness. If in a world given by the Creator, with trustworthy general principles behind things, a man can fall into deceit and error, it is because the will rushes ahead of knowledge, i.e. we do not consider all the facts before deciding upon a course of action or an opinion:

for as often as I so restrain my will within the limits of my knowledge, that it forms no judgement except regarding objects which are clearly and distinctly represented to it by the understanding, I can never be deceived; because every clear and distinct conception is doubtless something, and as such cannot owe its origin to nothing, but must of necessity have God for its author ...

(Meditation IV)

Day five: Of the essence of material things; and again, of god; that he exists

Descartes considers the general properties of material things, their quantity or extension in reality, utilizing such characteristics as length, breadth, depth and motion. They are also made up of many parts working together, and they are not simple, indivisible entities, unlike the soul or God. These quantities are self-evident in the mind, internally perceived as rational and necessary, even down to the concept of a triangle. The abstract fact of the three angles comes from within human reason, and not from seeing an actual triangle 'out there' in life.

God is perceived in such an internal manner, too, as a necessary Being. If God is perfect, then he must exist for Descartes, for perfection includes existing in reality. He rejects talk of distinguishing essence from existence or, we might say, pure concept and actual form/reality:

But, nevertheless, when I think of it more attentively, it appears that the existence can no more be separated from the essence of God than the idea of a mountain from that of a valley, or the equality of its three angles to two right angles, from the essence of a [rectilineal] triangle; so that it is not less impossible to conceive a God, that is, a being supremely perfect, to whom existence is awanting, or who is devoid of a certain perfection, than to conceive of a mountain without a valley ...

(Meditation V)

This is a form of the classical **ontological argument**, about which more in chapter Six.

> **KEYWORD**
>
> Ontological argument: the claim that if an idea of perfection can enter the human mind, then to be perfect, it must also exist in reality. Thus, if no greater Being than God can be imagined, there must be a God.

This might seem like highly abstract and circuitous reasoning, based upon the acceptance of certain presuppositions, but it was unshakeably clear and rational to Descartes. He argued that all inner, rational premises, 'clear and distinct' ideas as he called them, must be true: 'But although, in truth, I should be dreaming, the rule still holds that all which is clearly presented to my intellect is indisputably true.'

(Meditation V)

Day six: Of the existence of material things, and of the real distinction between the mind and nody of man

Descartes differentiates between conception (*intelligo*) and imagination, as an internal looking, a seeing with the eyes of the mind. Conception is the application of a faculty of the cogito (*facultas cognoscitiva*) when material objects are presented to it, an interaction, a dialogue, as it were. He speculates that he might form a clear and understandable concept of many-sided geometric shapes, such as a chiliogon with a thousand sides, but he cannot imagine this. Anything which can be imagined, such as a triangle or a pentagon, links to the world of material objects that are accessible through sense experience.

He recognizes that human beings have a faculty to receive sensual information, a passive faculty, and that these sensations are generally reliable, such as feeling hungry, heat and pain. True, the senses give partial information and might deceive us sometimes, such as when a square tower seems round from a distance. Though he admits that concrete objects might differ from his idea and interpretation of them through the senses, the general principles, the 'clear and distinct' ideas deduced in the mind, actually refer to things external to himself. Hence, his experience of having a particular body is seen as real and not imaginary.

He is careful to make a distinction between his perceptions and the objects themselves; thus fire produces the effect of heat in himself, but he cannot deduce that 'heat' and even 'pain' are internal properties of the fire itself. They are something that it produces in him. His body belongs to this external order experienced through the senses, being a mechanism of many parts, whereas his soul/mind is singular, sublime and undivided.

RESPONSES TO *THE MEDITATIONS*

The *Objections* revealed that many of his opponents had not understood his line of reasoning. They would often seize upon one of his absurd ideas which he had subsequently demolished, and portray it as an example of his errors. Descartes' most stringent replies were aimed at the *Seventh Set of Objections* by the Jesuit Pierre Bourdin. Bourdin took exception to the extreme form of scepticism which begins the First Meditation. This ignored Descartes own assertion that it was an extremely abstract, stylized form of doubt that he was using to find absolute certainty. He referred Bourdin to the closing section of *The Meditations* where he dismisses his earlier scepticism (such as the deceiving demon) as 'laughable'. Descartes appealed to the head of the Jesuit order in France, Father Dinet. In doing so, Descartes mentioned an earlier controversy over his views in his *Essays* at the University of Utrecht between his detractor Gisbert Voetius and his ally Henricus Reneri. This disputation had become vitriolic. Besides explaining his opponents misunderstandings in a published letter to Father Dinet, Descartes also appeals to the affirmative faith stance of his works. He claimed that it gave a better foundation for faith than the works of the Scholastics, and he also wrote to the Sorbonne saying that he did not wish to disturb any aspect of orthodox theology. Indeed, Descartes saw the existence of God and the soul as necessary for the scientific method to exist. Physics was knowledge perceived by the soul, and God guaranteed the existence of the physical world.

The Schoolmen were influenced by the Sceptics in so far as human beings are only capable of achieving a limited knowledge of the world. Only God knows all things. Thus they worked with a closed system of philosophy and scientific theory. We might call this lazy thinking, but a whole world-view and social order were dependent upon it. New ideas were challenges to the establishment.

KEY FACT
IRONY AND THE SCEPTICAL TRADITION

The Sceptics were a group of Greek thinkers who argued that we had little in the world that we could be certain of. This might be because everything kept on changing (such as the statement of Heraclitus c. 500 BCE that you can never step into the same river twice). The Sceptical tradition reached its apex with the Pyrrhonists, named after Pyrrho of Elis (c. 360–272 BCE). They taught at Plato's Academy in Athens and their views were popularized by the Roman Sextus Empiricus (c. 200 CE). The key point was that any real knowledge that we can attain is severely localized and limited. Appearances are relative and different people will have different angles on the truth. To have sure and certain knowledge, you must have something which all can agree upon before proceeding any further, a vital and robust sense of authority. Sextus was a doctor, and lived by a pragmatic common sense, never actually doubting that the real world ever existed. He worked from first impressions and past experiences.

It is often assumed that Descartes was following the Sceptics in looking at what could and could not be doubted. He writes as if he went through a sense of existential angst, a period of severe doubt about the possibility of knowledge. He might have done so, personally, or it might all be literary convention. Recent studies have pointed out that the Sceptics' methods were employed in disputations between the Jesuits and the Protestant Reformers, seeking absolute certainty and authority in faith and morals (the Church versus the Bible) and the one pilloried the views of the other, arguing that neither Church nor Scriptures could give the assured certainty that was sought after.

Was Descartes using this form of disputation to establish clear principles and foundations for the emerging scientific method, to show how order and reliable data could follow even when the world of the Scholastics was overturned? We have to leave that question open. Descartes was convinced he had found a sure point in the cogito and the existence of a good and perfect Deity.

✱ ✱ ✱ SUMMARY ✱ ✱ ✱

- Descartes was concerned to affirm Christian theology and faith and not to undermine it; he sought to undermine the system of the Schoolmen, though.

- *The Meditations* were written as a six-day reflection in the manner of the spiritual exercises of the time.

- Day one concerned the method of radical scepticism, doubting that anything should exist. Descartes even toys with the idea that all our perceptions and thoughts are influenced by a deceiving demon!

- Day two finds the answer to doubt in the cogito, our own thoughts and self-awareness.

- Day three argues for the existence of God to guarantee the truth of the world.

- Day four considers truth and error.

- Day five speaks of the nature of the extended, material world, and argues again for the existence of God to guarantee its laws and existence.

- Day six discusses the material creation and the difference between mind and body.

- Descartes was heavily criticized for what was considered an unhealthily exaggerated scepticism when he was using a literary device, probably in imitation of the Jesuits who were debating with the Protestants.

God 6

Belief in a perfect, good, eternal God and the immortality of the soul were central to Descartes' epistemology (theory of knowledge). The former guaranteed that the external world really existed and was not just a distortion of our senses, and the latter depended upon God's existence to have form, immortal nature and an innate ability to discern the fundamental principles of the universe. For Descartes, to have 'clear and distinct' ideas about reality, and the usefulness of mathematics, does not guarantee that they are telling the truth absolutely. Remember his fictitious deceiving demon, or the fact that he could be dreaming everything. It is only the existence of God that guarantees their reality, and this is because of a moral principle. If a good and perfect God exists, then such a Being would not trick and deceive the human mind about the 'clear and distinct' ideas. There really would be truth to discover out there. Thus, it is of vital importance that Descartes establishes proofs for God's existence.

PROVING THAT GOD EXISTS

Descartes provides two related 'proofs' of the existence of God in *The Meditations*:

* The idea of God in a human mind must have been given or revealed by the Supreme Being, for a finite mind could not conceive of an infinite thing.

* The idea of God demands that he exists, for a perfect being must have the property of existence to be perfect, just as a mountain cannot exist without a valley.

These kinds of proofs follow the ontological argument, one of the medieval classical proofs for the existence of God.

> **KEY FACT**
> **THE ONTOLOGICAL ARGUMENT**
>
> The ontological argument was framed by St Anselm (1033–1109). 'Ontological' is based on the Greek *ontos* meaning 'existence of being'. This follows the logical argument that if God is a perfect Being then God must exist, for perefection demands existence. An idea is inferior to something external and real.
>
> > We believe that God is a being than which none greater can be thought. Now even a fool knows that 'a being than which none greater can be thought' exists at least in his mind. But clearly, 'that than which a greater cannot be thought' cannot exist in the mind alone ... (Anselm, *Proslogion*, ch. 2)

THE CARTESIAN CIRCLE

Descartes added his own twist to the ontological argument as God was to be perceived by the mind as a 'clear and distinct' idea. For example, a triangle's angles must add up to 180 degrees to be a triangle, thus God had to exist to be a perfect being. The idea of God was as real and as clear as his own sense of being a thinking self. The clear and distinct idea of God was logically coherent and demanded that he actually existed. This whole argument becomes circular, and Descartes' position has been called 'the Cartesian Circle'. His contemporary critic, Antoine Arnauld (1612–94) was the first to point out the circularity of his argument. If the 'clear and distinct' ideas depend upon God's existence to be real and trustworthy, and if God's existence can be proved by his perception as a 'clear and distinct' idea, then we are going round and round in circles, using one premise to establish another. This is a case that if p (a proposition), then p is so. It is not always clear if Descartes means us to think that we first have to know clear and distinct ideas, and then recognize God as such, and thus know he is real, or that God's being guarantees the existence of the clear and distinct ideas.

Some subsequent commentators believe that Descartes was merely using God to validate the *memory* of proofs, or clear and distinct ideas. Thus, when you had the flash of inspiration, the moment of clarity when the pattern fell into place and you 'saw' with the mind's eye the proof, the rules of the equation or whatever, you did not need anything to validate this. It was self-evidently true. Later, when memory fades and you cannot recall the logical steps, the existence of God guarantees the truth of the proposition. His order has established such a universe where clear and distinct ideas are possible. God becomes a short cut or an ultimate epistemological insurance policy.

Another commentator's twist is to see God as guaranteeing the reality of clear and distinct ideas, and thereby dispensing with any need for knowledge of the logic that establishes the clear and distinct ideas. This is akin to using a car and not necessarily knowing how it works, or switching on a light and not having a clue about the electrics. There can be an assumption that if we cannot logically articulate something, then it is incoherent. Socrates loved to interrogate his audience and get them to explain terms such as 'bravery' or 'justice'. They could not, but their actions were clearly those of the brave or the just or whatever. Our perceiving mind might well operate by a whole set of rules of logical principles that transform sensory input into concepts, but we can have the concepts without the understanding of how they are formed – and they still have sense and currency!

CAUSAL ADEQUACY

Descartes also used the Scholastic notion of the Causal Adequacy Principle. This taught that there was a hierarchy of being, whereby causes were as real as their effects, and things that physically exist are more real than things just in the mind. Thus, the idea of God is caused by God the Creator, placing knowledge of himself in the minds of his creations. (This is sometimes known as the trademark argument, as a designer stamps his or her mark on what he or she makes.) Also, once we have the idea of God in our heads, he must really exist, for external existence is superior to mental ideas. **Causal adequacy** could be refined further to state that the **hierarchy of being** displayed the following levels:

> **KEYWORDS**
>
> Causal adequacy: causes are as real as their effects.
>
> Hierarchy of being: there is a chain of being, whereby some things are more real than others, the infinite more real than the finite and so on.

* infinite substance
* finite substance
* attributes of a finite substance
* modes of being of a finite substance
* ideas.

We see, also, the idea that a cause passes on something of itself to its effect. Movement produces motion. The idea of x shares the nature of the property of x. Reality is not always so clear cut, and some causes produce effects that do not seem to be obviously related – such as electricity formed by iron in a magnetic field. Does the idea of God demand God's existence anymore than the idea of infinity demand an infinite existence? Perhaps it does, but it is not logically demanded. Descartes was still very much immersed in his time, subverting the Scholastics, but still thinking their thoughts.

WHAT CAN WE MAKE OF THE ONTOLOGICAL ARGUMENT?

Once we move away from the Scholastic reasoning, the ontological argument sounds less and less convincing. Even in Anselm's time, the monk Gaunilo mocked the idea by saying that you could think anything into existence by this premise, such as the perfect paradise island! Immanuel Kant (1724–1804) refused to see existence as a simple predicate of God, unlike 'goodness' and 'omnipotence'. God's existence could not so easily be assumed as a given; it had to be proved. As Kant put it, money in his mind did not produce money in his wallet. The other classical proofs need to be engaged, such as the cosmological and teleological arguments, seeing evidence for God in the design and purpose of the universe, or the moral argument, whereby human beings all have a conscience and a set of ethical beliefs.

KEY FACT
THE CLASSICAL PROOFS OF GOD

Apart from Anselm's ontological argument, here are three others:

* The cosmological argument – this an a-posteriori argument, arguing from what is given, or from below. This states that the cosmos requires an Unmoved Mover, or a First Cause. Each changing, moving thing requires a cause, but there must be an undergirding Ultimate Cause.

* The teleological argument – *telos* means 'end', and this idea asserts that not only has the cosmos come from somewhere, but it has a purpose, a destiny. This can sometimes be called the argument from design, for the orderliness of the cosmos demands that there be a Creator, giving it direction and purpose.

* The moral argument – Kant dismissed the above arguments but held to a sense of conscience and ethical awareness across ages and cultures as a sign that we were made in God's image. There is a universal sense of moral obligation, and this ought he called the *categorical imperative*.

These 'proofs' are not actually so watertight. They are more like arguments or suggestions. The idea of a First Cause can be dismissed if one believes in an eternally evolving universe that operates by the principle of infinite regression, for example. There is just no end to the succession of cause and effect. The moral argument does not do enough justice to the difference in ethical stances across ages and cultures, even if some universals can be established.

ULTIMATE REALITY, OR DEPTH?

Other thinkers have tried to rehabilitate the ontological argument, such as the theologian Paul Tillich (1886–1965) who defined God as 'Ultimate Reality'. No one could deny that reality exists, though we might differ over our definitions of it. Perhaps if Anselm is paraphrased to, 'We believe that there is a depth to life and an ultimate purpose than which none greater can be thought', then we can be face to face with the mystery of existence in all its rawness. Descartes' edifices of belief and epistemology are another matter. They depend upon a position of faith to begin with. If one has the gift of faith, then trust in a perfect and good God can assure us of the trustation of our ideas and of the existence of external reality.

THE GOD OF THE PHILOSOPHERS

Descartes claimed to be writing a defence of fundamental Christian truths and he was dismayed to find the Jesuits turning against him. He said that his teachings left matters of orthodox theology undisturbed. He did not discuss the details and specific doctrines, but laid the foundations for the assured existence of God and the soul at a time of doubt and a jettisoning of the older Scholastic world-view. Thus he could claim in a letter to theologians at the Sorbonne that he bolstered the faith rather than attacked it. It can be said that Descartes' God is far more abstract than the God worshipped by believers. He is a far cry from the God of the Bible or of personal experience. Blaise Pascal (1623–62) was a renowned mathematician of the same period as Descartes, but he was to find renewed faith through religious experience in 1654. This was more immediate and trustworthy than the God of the philosophers:

> From about half past ten in the evening until about half past midnight.
> Fire.
> God of Abraham, God of Isaac, God of Jacob, not of the philosophers and scholars. Certainty, certainty, heartfelt, joy, peace.
> God of Jesus Christ ...
> The world forgotten, and everything except God ...
> Joy, joy, joy, tears of joy.
>
> (Pascal, *Pensées*)

Perhaps there is no escape from faith for any type of believer. The intellectual defence and apparatus of Descartes still required a premise of faith that accepted the reality of God. Once this was taken as a given, it could provide a security.

KEY FACT
PIETISTS AND JANSENISTS

The seventeenth century saw different attempts to establish a place for Christianity and faith in the midst of the rise of science and Rationalism. Pietism began in the German Lutheran Church as a reaction against its stress of doctrinal orthodoxy. Personal experience and grace where to be emphasized. A faith should be a living faith.

In the Catholic Church, Saint-Cyran Duvergier (1581–1643) and Cornelius Jansen (1585–1638) developed the teaching that the experience of divine grace was needed to be able to perform any good or holy work. Antoine Arnauld was involved with this movement, as was Pascal. This experiential, personalist strand also gave rise to movements such as Methodism in the eighteenth century. The term 'pietist' has come to mean a withdrawal from intellectual disputes and political action, perhaps not always fairly.

GOD AND MOTION

For Descartes, God is essential to allow finite things to exist and, even more, to allow motion and change in the position of material objects. He rejected the teaching of the Schoolmen, following on from Aristotle, that each finite object had an inner substance from which all its properties could be deduced, hence fire rises and apples fall from trees. He replaced the substances with God himself. God is the ground or guarantor of all things. God is seen as the conserver in Descartes idea of continual re-creation. As he writes in *The Meditations*:

> so that from the fact that I existed a short time ago, it does not follow that I ought to exist now, unless some cause creates me again as it were in this moment, that is, conserves me.
>
> (Meditation III)

As we are finite and imperfect, then that power cannot be innate within us otherwise we could will perfection for ourselves. It must reside in God as the supreme and perfect Being. In his *Principles of Philosophy*, he writes:

> We also understand that there is perfection in God not only because He is Himself immutable, but also because He works in the most constant and immutable way.
>
> (Principles of Philosophy II)

In Descartes' writings, God's continuous re-creation can be understood according to two different models. One is a continuous stream of new acts of creation which result in motion. This has been compared to a film strip of recurring images, a divine zoetrope. This was the **Occasionalist** doctrine, whereby motion is actually and directly caused by God re-creating objects at different points. Any secondary causes are 'occasional' and not the real cause of motion.

> **KEYWORD**
>
> Occasionalist: someone who believes that God directly causes motion, and secondary effects from impact of bodies are mere 'occasions', by-products of God's will-in-action. Some thinkers saw God as continuously re-creating objects from moment to moment in different points in space.

Another model presents itself and distances Descartes from the Occasionalists. This is that God provides an impulse that produces motion, just as our minds can move our bodies. God is continually affecting material objects but this allows that there could be other things providing impulses, especially the human mind. This latter model is more fruitful when considering the relationship between mind, body and the world of extended reality, as will be discussed later.

God is the agent of causation in the world. How, exactly, Descartes envisaged God doing this is open to debate, as is the question of whether any derivative causes can be traced to material objects. Thus a billiard ball hitting another can be said to cause motion by its impact, but does God directly will this, or allow it to be possible by the way the universe is made? The latter idea would have God putting properties into his creation which cannot be changed, including an amount of motion between things. Billiard balls can only move in a certain way because that is how they are made. This would place God behind the laws of motion as their ultimate author and source, rather than directly willing them. Some of Descartes ideas are opaque and open to question, such as this passage from a letter to Henry More:

That transference that I call motion is a thing of no less entity than shape is, namely, it is a mode in a body. However the force moving a body can be that of God conserving as much transference in matter as he placed in it at the first moment of creation ...

Another matter open to debate is how far Descartes believed that finite minds (or angels, for that matter) could cause motion in external objects, and more elusively, whether objects could affect the mind by causing sensations (or did God do it?). These debates must be set in the context of the views of many of Descartes followers and the views of Occasionalism. These stated that the only cause of motion in the world was God, acting and willing directly. There was no room for any finite agent of motion. Thus, Louis de la Forge could write in *Œuvres Philosophiques*:

> I hold that there is no creature, spiritual or corporeal, that can change [the position of a body] or that of any of its parts in the second instant of its creation if the creator does not do it Himself ...

Descartes was more complex and subtle than some of his followers allowed.

CONTACT THEORY

However exactly Descartes understood God causing motion, both he and subsequent thinkers adopted a view of impact or contact that implied the activity of God or the mind directly upon objects. There was a 'hands on' approach. Why does the apple fall to the ground? Because God willed it. As observations suggested regular laws or patterns of behaviour in the natural world, God began to recede further and further away. The **reductio ad absurdum** comes with the idea of 'the God of the gaps' whereby only what cannot be explained in terms of rational forces is the work of God. This means that God fades like the

KEYWORD

Reductio ad absurdum: a reduction to the absurd, taking an argument to its most extreme and absurd level.

Cheshire Cat's grin in *Alice in Wonderland*. The principle of **Ockham's razor** removes that which is superfluous to an argument, and God is cut away as an unnecessary speculation. When the naturalist, Laplace, presented his theories to Napoleon, he asked what place he had for God in his system. The reply came: 'Sire, I have no need of such a hypothesis.'

> **KEYWORD**
>
> Ockham's Razor: a principle used by William of Ockham (c. 1287–1347) whereby unnecessary facts or arguments are stripped away. Often summarized as 'If in doubt, take the simplest explanation.'

Contact theory has plagued the debate between science and religion ever since. Thus, for example, a scientist such as Richard Dawkins is able to propose a purely materialist understanding of life:

> But when the ricochets of atomic billiards chance to put together an object that has a certain, seemingly innocent property, something momentous happens in the universe. That property is an ability to self-replicate; that is, the object is able to use the surrounding materials to make exact copies of itself, including replicas of such minor flaws in copying as may occasionally arise. What will follow from this singular occurrence, anywhere in the universe, is Darwinian selection and hence the baroque extravaganza that, on this planet, we call life.
>
> (Dawkins, *River Out of Eden*)

Theologians of the Enlightenment however saw God as undergirding the laws of physics, creating them in the first place and then letting them get on with the job. This model, in turn, has its limitations. It is like Paley's watch. God creates a machine and lets it tick away.

KEY FACT
PALEY'S WATCH

William Paley, the Archdeacon of Carlisle, proposed in 1802 that finding a stone on the path might allow him to think it had been there forever. However, upon finding a watch, when we examine it we find that its several parts had been put together for a purpose. The watch must have had a maker. So, too, must the world.

The New Physics suggests that the cosmos is not a machine, but a dynamic and evolving affair that is often random. Neither is an object ever actually at rest – at a sub-atomic level it is a dance of atoms. Perhaps God can be found within the processes as an influencing agent but not a direct causal agent. Process theologians, for example, have a bipolar concept of the deity. God is beyond and within his creation, as a playwright can act in his own play. The actual freedom granted to the cosmos is at play with God and he seeks to guide it, almost as a Lover and a Beloved. As John V. Taylor put it in *The Go-Between God*:

> God is really on the inside, we must find him in the processes, not in the gaps. We know now there are no gaps, no points at which a special intervention is conceiveable.

Theology tries to speak credibly today of divine influence in a sub-atomic, quantum universe of many levels and dimensions beyond those of length, breadth and height which can be measured conventionally. Law's are observations of the normal, regular pattern of events which might be placed there by God but his hand is not directly involved in every event. A primitive, bare contact theory leads to a rational cul-de-sac.

SO WHAT DID DESCARTES BELIEVE?

Descartes followed Aquinas in differentiating two sorts of cause, the **causa secundum fieri** and the **causa secundum esse**. These can be translated as 'a cause of becoming' and 'a cause of being'. Basically, the former means that the effect of the causal agent is still in operation even though the agent has ceased to act. This would be akin to an architect who builds a house. Once it is finished, he rolls up his plans and goes home, but the fruits of his labours still stand.

> **KEYWORDS**
>
> Causa secundum fieri: a cause of becoming. The effects of the causal agent continue.
>
> Causa secundum esse: a cause of being. Once an act is completed, its effects cease, unless they are continuously repeated.

The latter idea suggests that the casual agent must continue to act for its effect to continue, such as the sun continues shining to allow its light to be. Descartes sees God as this kind of causal agent, a *causa secundum esse*. God must carry on acting to conserve creation; the cosmos is not a totally independent machine that God created once upon a time:

> the sun is the cause of the light proceeding from it, and God is the cause of created things, not only as a cause of becoming, but as a cause of being, and therefore must always flow into the effect in the same way, in order to conserve it.
>
> (Reply to *Fifth Objections*)

Descartes, in fact, follows Aquinas on these points (as in Aquinas' *Summa Theologiae*).

It might be the case that Aquinas' God conserves immaterial substances that give form, properties and motion to objects, whilst Descartes removes substances and places God directly in the cosmos. He was still influenced by some of this terminology, though. He argued that the mind–body relationship was the only valid type of substance. He often used the Scholastic idea of heaviness (learnt by school pupils) to elucidate his ideas of mind–body interaction. He even argued that the Scholastic substances were quasi-sentient:

> heaviness bore bodies toward the centre of the earth as if it contained in itself some knowledge of it (i.e., the centre of the earth). For this could not happen without knowledge, and there cannot be any knowledge except in a mind ...
>
> (from his letter to Regius, 1642)

Descartes seems to differentiate two types of causal effects in God, that of sustainer and that of modal causes. Sustaining is an undergirding power in the background, modal causation is a direct intervention or 'shove'. Matter can be conserved without this modal impulse, but they will be at rest. The impulse moves them.

Descartes saw mind–body interaction as the existential paradigm for understanding all causation – rather than the forms or substances of the Schoolmen, it was God who was at work within his creation. He refused to go down the line of reductionist mechanism.

✳ ✳ ✳ SUMMARY ✳ ✳ ✳

- God was the guarantor of reality for Descartes.

- The ontological argument sought the proof of God's reality in the fact that the idea of the Supreme Being was implanted in our minds (also known as the trademark argument).

- The Cartesian circle is the idea that having one thing proves the other.

- Descartes worked within the idea of causal adequacy and the idea of a hierarchy of being. Causes were as real as their effects, and physical realities were more real than ideas.

- Modern theologians debate the value of the ontological argument. Perhaps there is vitality in the fact that humanity has the idea of God in their minds, and harbours a spiritual quest and vision, needing to worship something. We experience depth issues and questions of Ultimate Concern.

- The God of the philosophers was different from the God of the Bible, as shown by Pascal's conversion and passionate, experiential belief.

- Descartes spent a great deal of energy on the question of motion and causation. Occasionalists saw God as directly causing each movement, or even as re-creating an object from moment to moment at a different point in space and time. Descartes gave room for the human mind and angels to cause motion in bodies, and seems to have seen God's involvement in a twofold manner. First, God set certain properties in physical objects that determine how they can move (which would later be called laws) and then God influences them by impulses just as our minds move our bodies.

7 The Soul

The terms 'mind' and 'soul' are interchangeable in Descartes' works. They are a translation of the French *l'me* (soul) and *l'esprit* (mind/spirit). The soul for Descartes was fundamentally a thinking substance, *res cogitans*. This was the only aspect of existence which we can be sure of, that we are a thinking person. We are conscious beings. *Cogito, ergo sum*.

> But immediately, I noticed that while I was trying in this way to think that everything was false, it was necessary that I, who was thinking this, was something. And observing this truth, 'I am thinking, therefore I exist' was so firm and sure that even the most extravagant suppositions of the sceptics were incapable of shaking it, I decided to accept without scruple as the first principle of the philosophy I was seeking …
>
> (*Discourse on the Method*, Part IV)

The soul was a thing of itself, indivisible unlike the body (with arms, legs, etc.) and not like *extended reality* with its quantities of length, breadth and height. It could not be measured.

> Next, I examined attentively what I was. I saw that while I could pretend I had no body and that there was no world and no place for me to be in, I could not for all that pretend that I did not exist … From this I recognized that I was a substance whose whole essense or nature is solely to think, and which does not require any place, or depend on any material thing, in order to exist. Accordingly this 'I' – that is, the soul by which I am what I am – is entirely distinct from the body, and indeed, is easier to know than the body, and would not cease to be everything it is even if the body did not exist.
>
> (*Discourse on the Method*, Part IV)

It was superior and spiritual by virtue of its ability to perceive 'clear and distinct' ideas, and was only just down the rung of existence from God himself. This was a leaning towards Plato away from Aristotle, whereby that which belonged to the world of the timeless, rational and abstract was more real and enduring. The world of Ideals stood behind and above that of changeable Forms.

GHOST IN THE MACHINE?

This radical separation of mind and body is known as Cartesian dualism and seems extreme and problematical. Does it not make the body a mere automaton? The term 'ghost in the machine' was coined by the Oxford philosopher Gilbert Ryle (1900–76) to capture this sense of radical dualism.

Descartes wrestled with the problem and recognized profound links between mind and body. He did not see the soul as trapped in a body, contrary to many popular views of his thought. There was a dynamic link, a real, substantial union or interdependence. It is not like a force operating a machine, as though we drive a car. We feel pain, the 'I' in my head hurts.

> Nature also teaches me, by these sensations of pain, hunger, thirst and so on, that I am not merely present in my body as a sailor is present in a ship, but that I am very closely joined and, as it were, intermingled with it, so that I and the body form a unit.
>
> (Sixth Meditation, IV)

The Fourth Set of Objections to *The Meditations* has Antoine Arnauld asserting:

> It seems that the argument [that the mind can exist apart from the body] proves too much, and takes us back to the Platonic view … that man is merely a rational soul, and the body merely a vehicle to the soul …

This was to accuse Descartes of Platonic angelism.

Descartes replied to the objection that he taught 'a soul which makes use of a body' thus:

> I thought I was very careful to guard against anyone inferring that a human being is simply 'a soul which makes use of a body'. For in the Sixth Meditation, where I dealt with the distinction between the mind and the body, I also proved at the same time that the mind is substantially united with the body. And the arguments which I have used to prove this are as strong as any I can remember having read …

KEY FACT
ONE, TWO OR THREE?

Descartes argues that we are human beings composed of a soul and a body. The soul and body form a unique and profound unity when joined: the human being. We are psychosomatic unities. But what reality does the state of union have, and how does soul affect body?

Descartes conceded that a part of the body was separable from the rest of the bodily parts, and from the soul, but that it belonged to the nature of the whole man. The mind might exist apart from the body, but it is 'substantially united' with it. He might also speak of the soul as an 'entity in its own right' and the body as 'an accidental entity', but there was a union. It is difficult to assess Descartes here, for he seems to want things both ways. The soul is of a superior order of being and is distinct, surviving the death of the body, but it is also united to the body. His disciple, Regius, argued that the human being was merely an accidental entity when a soul is united to a body, an *ens per accidens*. Descartes was quick to refute him, saying: 'You could scarcely have said anything more objectionable and provocative.' He wrote to him later on, spelling out that the human being was an *ens per se*, an entity in its own right:

> The mind is united in a real and substantial manner to the body … For if an angel were in a human body, it would not have sensations as we do, but would simply perceive the motions which are caused by external objects, and in this way would differ from a genuine human being.

Thus, it can be said that Descartes had a real anthropology, a sense of *being human*.

> **KEY FACT**
> **ROYAL CORRESPONDENCE**
>
> Descartes corresponded with the Princess Elizabeth of Bohemia, and his replies reveal a great deal about his struggle with the mind/body problem. He worked with a model of three aspects to the human being – the intellectual (mind), the extended (the body) and the passions (resulting from the union of the other two). This trialism might suggest a move away from his radical dualism but, upon closer examination, the first two aspects are preserved as substantive and irreducible. The third is dependent upon them, and thus *attributive* and not *substantive*.

PRIMITIVE NOTION

Princess Elizabeth of Bohemia wrote to Descartes in 1642 asking how, if the soul were a separate substance from the body, it could exert influence over it. How could an incorporeal thing control the movement of a corporeal object? Descartes replied that he was only trying to show that there was a distinction between mind and body, but there was a union, a union that was experienced in everyday experience and common sense. It could not be explained, and was, indeed, what he referred to as a 'primitive notion', meaning a concept that could not be reduced further. Thus, he posited three primitive notions in the human being, mind/body/union. The union was found in the emotions, for hunger was felt and could not be reduced or separated into the intellectual realization of the need for food or the contracting stomach muscles. There was sensation and personal feeling. The experience of hunger demands being fully conscious and alert. If we are drugged so that we do not feel pain, or unconscious and not aware of our needs, then something is missing.

Descartes wrote in his second letter to Elizabeth;

> Metaphysical thoughts, which exercise the pure intellect, help to familiarize us with the notion of the soul; and the study of mathematics, which exercises mainly the imagination in the consideration of shapes and motions, accustoms us to form very distinct notions of body. But it is the ordinary course of life and conversation, and abstention from meditation and from the study of things which exercise the imagination, that teaches us how to conceive the union of the soul and the body ...

In other words, common sense teaches us that we are a single entity called a human being. We perceive the union by living. He seems to be saying that we should not seek to analyse this union; it is a given, as is the mind and the body. Some have criticized him for calling the union a primitive notion. This suggests that it cannot be broken down any further, but it is an effect of two things and perhaps not a thing in itself. It is rather like saying that water is a primitive notion when it is actually composed of other substances (H_2O). However, its quality as 'watery' is unique to its state, and this might be akin to Descartes' third category of the union. As a derivative effect, it is unique and distinctive, even though it depends upon mind + body. Its properties are irreducible.

SENSING AND REPRESENTING

For Descartes, the soul could act and be acted upon. There was an interaction with the body and the external world. He refined this by saying that the senses only impacted the soul, they did not actually represent objects. The soul made the representations as it responded to the senses. The Scholastic ideas had the intellect perceiving the object and the senses representing the categories or attributes – this is a melon; the melon is yellow and sweet. Descartes had the soul perceiving the whole thing – the senses impact the soul with a sweet, yellow melon.

Descartes speculated that the rational soul was joined to the body through the pineal gland in the brain. The senses impacted this and motions produced within this stimulated the soul into forming ideas and representations.

THE PASSIONS OF THE SOUL

Descartes last work, *The Passions of the Soul*, published in 1649, explored the mind–body union further, acknowledging the vitality and necessity of the emotions. We do not live a detached, austere, abstract intellectual life but a *human* life. Here we are said to be more than mere *res cogitans*. He points out how bodily functions combine with intellectual thoughts and produce the passions, movements of blood around the heart as we fall in love, a dryness of the throat as we feel thirst and so on. He concludes that the reason is superior to the passions, though, and must master them without suppressing and denying them. Just as irrational animals can be trained, so can our passions be:

> But the true function of reason in the conduct of life is to examine and consider without passion the value of all the perfections, both of body and of the soul, which can be acquired by our conduct, so that since we are commonly obliged to deprive ourselves of some goods in order to acquire others, we shall always choose the better.
>
> (Letter to Elizabeth, 1 September 1645)

CAN THE MIND AFFECT THE PHYSICAL?

Descartes' ideas about God and causation were presented in the preceding chapter. The Occasionalists refused to allow that the mind could cause any motion in external objects, even in the body. All was directly willed by God. Descartes did seem to allow that the mind/soul did have a power to produce motion, even though it was finite. In fact, he used the mind's ability to move the body as an analogy for the influence of the divine on inanimate objects. When writing to Henry More in 1649 he asserted:

> I confess, nevertheless, that I can find no idea in my mind which represents the way in which God or an angel can move matter, which is different from the idea that shows me the way in which I am conscious that I can move my own body through my thought.

Again, in his letter to Arnauld in 1648, he writes:

> That the mind, which is incorporeal, can set a body in motion is shown to us every day by the most certain and most evident experience, without the need of any reasoning or comparison with anything else.

The mind had a real, innate power to affect the external world in so far as it was incorporeal. He allowed the power of the mind, exercised through the gift of free will, to affect changes in the world, though these changes had to be in accord to God's principles of creation that were in-built into extended reality, including the amount of motion an object could possess. How far could our actions be said to be in line with the will of God?

In one of his letters to Elizabeth of Bohemia he seeks to console her when she fears that God can only give hope when considering the courses of nature as he is their author, but not when considering the free (and cruel) actions of mortals. Descartes replies that since God is perfect, then he cannot allow anything to exist in his world that would be against his will:

> God is the universal cause of everything in such a way that He is in the same way the total cause of everything, and thus nothing can happen without His will.

This seems to deride free will, and it opens a typical theological conundrum. How can we be free if what we choose is God's will? Did God will the Holocaust, then? Theologians might qualify this by saying that God might allow things to be, without directly willing them. Modern theology is more open to the randomness of the universe and the necessary distance God puts between it and himself, an 'epistemic' distance.

CAN BODIES AFFECT THE MIND?

A further consideration asks if a material object can be a causal agent of sensation in the mind. In his earlier Meditations, Descartes had written:

> Now there is in me a certain passive faculty for sensing, that is, a faculty for receiving and knowing the ideas of sensible things. But I could not make use of it unless a certain active faculty for producing or bringing about those ideas were either in me or in something else.
>
> (*Meditation*, VI)

This 'something else' can be a material body, God, or some other incorporeal form. This ascribes genuine causation to objects. His later *Principles of Philosophy* soften this claim:

> We seem to ourselves clearly to see that its idea comes from things placed outside of us.
>
> (*Principles*, II)

Perhaps he was allowing that God had to be actively involved in producing the sensation in the mind when faced with an external object. This is a matter of some debate, but as Descartes seems to accept that all inanimate motion is caused by God, then it would be surprising to allow an exception in the cause of sensation. But is the passive, inner faculty the receiver and thus the framer of the sensation rather than the external thing?

END THOUGHTS

Descartes posits a radical dualism only to sew the mind and body back again, admitting mysteries and puzzles that cannot really be answered. His critics such as Antoine Arnauld, in his own lifetime, were not convinced that he had proved that the soul was so separable from the body, and the 'self' was really so ethereal. The body is still essential to what makes a human being as well as the soul. Common sense declares that we are mind *and* body, as even Descartes had to allow. Descartes' assertion of the third primitive notion acts as a lacuna as we see a disjunction in concepts that strains to form something beyond current categories of conceptualization. The either/or of binary opposition breaks down and we see a yes/no, a both/and. This is always a sign that there are mysteries afoot, and that reality is far more complex than we have so far allowed. Are 'mind' and 'body' our categorizations and abstractions for the deep mystery of human being?

Also, critics since Descartes wonder if the soul is as indivisible as he thought, for what link to the brain does it really have? If the brain and nervous system were damaged, would the 'I' still be in my head? Whatever the mind might be, there is the abiding and irreducible mystery of conscious perception and personal awareness. We are present to ourselves and not only to others external from us. If mental perceptions only correspond to physical sensations, then it is still amazing and puzzling that we can think and feel. What is the 'I' in our heads?

KEY FACT
QUALIA – THE STATE OF EXPERIENCE AND FEELING
Can physical science adequately analyse the *qualia* of human existence – can it ever really encompass the beauty we feel when faced with a stunning sunrise, or a new baby's first smile? If we argue that a sentence can be weighed by measuring the chemicals produced in the brain and the electrical impulses as it is thought and/or spoken, that does not really get inside it and consider the abstract level of its human meaning.

Descartes leaves us the legacy of realizing that human beings have levels that are baffling, unique and mysterious. We might even call these 'spiritual', no matter what exact definition we give to that term. His terms of reference and methods of analysis might be debated and superseded in some ways; he might have left many unanswered questions and refused to analyse adequately the state of the union and the entity it produces, but there is no way of completely exorcizing the 'ghost' from the 'machine'. Dualism exerts a fundamental appeal that has not died a total conceptual death.

✻ ✻ ✻ SUMMARY ✻ ✻ ✻

- The cogito is basically a thinking substance, a *res cogitans*.

- Cartesian views have been criticized as believing in a 'ghost in the machine'. If the mind is totally separate, how can it influence the body?

- Descartes rejected charges of angelism and sought to elucidate a sublime union between mind and body that resulted in the human being.

- In his correspondence with Elizabeth of Bohemia, he declared that the mind and body were both primitive notions, as was the union. A primitive notion is a concept that cannot be broken down any further.

- He was a thoroughgoing Rationalist when discussing mental representations. The soul forms representations out of the impacts with bodies.

- He admitted a vital role for the emotions in human life, but sought to temper and control them by reason.

- He saw the mind as being able to influence the body directly, contra to the Occasionalists, but it was less clear how the body might affect the mind. He seemed to leave the matter open for the possibility that God intervened to form sensations in the mind.

8 'Beast-Machines': Descartes and animals

ANIMALS AS AUTOMATA?
Descartes' elevation of the human soul above the body led him to believe that animals were non-rational and had no form of soul. They were purely forms of extended reality. From this it is usually deduced that he did not believe that they could actually feel pain – they just acted as if they did. Thus, a dog with an injured paw whimpered not in conscious pain but because it was mechanically malfunctioning. They could not experience pain if they had no self-consciousness. The sounds were just noises as the machine was taken apart and stopped functioning. This is the common assumption and charge against him, and the evils of industrialization and the rupture of our place in the environment are laid at his feet.

The fact that he was fascinated with dissection to see how animals worked, often visiting butchers shops and taking chunks of animal carcasses home, had added to the air of malevolence. Here, he was just being a faithful student, as doctors dissected human corpses and we should not read anything macabre into it. It is important to test what Descartes actually did believe about animals. This reveals his ideas about mind/body more clearly.

THE BÊTE-MACHINE
The 'animal-machine' idea of Descartes is open to interpretation. Critics have broken down this doctrine into several component parts:

* Animals are machines.

* Animals are automata (i.e. they can move of their own accord).

* Animals do not think.

'Beast-Machines': Descartes and animals

- Animals possess no language.
- Animals have no self-consciousness.
- Animals do not have consciousness.
- Animals do not feel pain.

The last point in particular is absurd and monstrous. Descartes definitely held some of these propositions but perhaps not all of them. He might have held the first five propositions, but he definitely did not hold to the final point. He did not really hold to the sixth, either, as shall be explained.

MERE AUTOMATA?

Descartes did say that animals were machines, as in one of his letters to More:

> all the motions of animals originate from the corporeal and mechanical principle …

He also stated that the human body was a machine in just the same way, and his language of mechanisms must be understood in the context of his philosophy of material things, of extended reality, which could be reduced to and understood to operate by, mathematical principles. To describe something as mechanical does not necessary exclude feeling. It is true that human beings also have a soul, which makes a difference.

The term **automaton** was used by Descartes as in his correspondence with More:

> it seems reasonable that since art copies nature, and men can make various automata which move without thought, that nature should produce its own automata much more splendid than the artificial ones. These natural automata are the animals.

KEYWORD

Automaton: literally an object that is self-moving. This might or might not imply consciousness. It need not mean a 'mere machine'.

He uses the term 'automaton' in the Greek sense of 'self-moving object', and, again, this does not necessarily rule out any sense of feeling. The soul was described by other philosophers of the time as a kind of 'spiritual automaton' as it had a vitality of its own.

NOT THINKING AND SPEAKING

An automaton could never be mistaken for a man, no matter how cleverly made, for it could not speak rationally. While it is true that a parrot can be trained to speak, or dogs and cats communicate in barks and mews, these are never stimulus-free events. They are not adequate, rational language that can form words and concepts and freely respond to another. Such a being does not 'arrange its speech in various ways in order to reply appropriately to everything that could be said in its presence'.

Descartes uses terms such as *cogitare* or *penser* as the functions of the rational soul which include will and every other faculty. Thinking includes 'all the operations of the soul'. This does not necessarily mean that only a being with a rational soul can feel. *Cogito, ergo sum* implies self-awareness and the reflective ability. An animal might see without this being a self-reflective experience.

Writing to More, he goes on to describe animal communication as 'their natural impulses of anger, fear, hunger and so on'. In other correspondence, he refers to training animals to imitate human sounds. All these things merely communicate their need for attention or food: 'Similarly, all the things which dogs, horses and monkeys are made to do are merely expressions of their fear, their hope, or their joy; and consequently, they can do these things without any thought.' Thus, Descartes does not deny that animals have feelings!

To make matters clearer, Descartes separated *cogitatio* (thinking) from *sensus* (sensation), stating to More that 'I deny sensation to no animal …'.

CONSCIOUS, BUT NOT SELF-SO

Descartes grouped animals into the mass of extended reality and, on one level, would see their movements and their noises as the result of natural mechanisms that made them operate. Thus hunger in an animal might be no more than the contraction of certain muscles. An animal might not be self-aware, reflectively, of the pain, but it does cry out in pain. It does not suffer in silence. This suggests consciousness, but not the fully developed self-consciousness of a human being. Commentators accuse Descartes of a certain fuzziness of thought at this point. He could describe the experience of animal emotions in humans as operations of the blood, brain, muscles and so forth, as well as purely intellectual/spiritual appreciations. Can emotions such as hope really be separable into the animal and the intellectual? If an animal can show hope, then it has an intellectual aspect to some extent. Descartes might not have been the thoroughgoing dualist that he is claimed to be. We do not only notice that we are hungry; we feel it. There is a link between mind and body which drove him to postulate a third primitive notion and a mind–body unity that produced the uniquely human state of being. Thus, he denies the charge of angelism by stating that an angel in a human body would not feel the things that affected that body. It would merely note that they were happening.

Where do the animals fit in? They are also immediately aware of being in pain, or of experiencing joy or hope, but at a far less sophisticated, reflective level than are we.

AND TODAY?

We are now more aware of human evolution and the gradual emergence of human consciousness from simpler forms. Lower species have their own form of mind, and some species are very close to us, such as apes and dolphins. Philosophers now describe human language as an *emergence* from the more basic communications of animals which serve as warning signals which needs such as hunger communicating and sounds of non-threatening acceptance. There is something other, more, advanced, sublime about human discourse.

Whatever sense is made of the term 'soul' today, animals do share in a level of consciousness and in life. They are living beings, and those with more advanced brains and nervous systems ascend the scale of sentience. The theologians might squabble and speculate about their eternal destiny, but common sense and biological investigations show that they are in the same chain of being as ourselves.

Descartes' dependence on certain Scholastic ideas could have led him in a different direction, ironically. The hierarchy of being could have allowed animals to possess a lesser form of reason or soul in a progression had Descartes thought that way. He saw himself as midway between God and Nothingness. Animals could have had a vital place within that scheme beneath him but not reduced to the level of machines in the field of extended reality. Still, Descartes' views are exaggerated and often misrepresented. There was more linking us with the beasts in his thought than many imagine. It might be the case that distortions of his views and the radical dualism of some of his followers led to beastliness to the beasts, and to the earth, but Descartes was not guilty of this himself.

✷ ✷ ✷ SUMMARY ✷ ✷ ✷

- Descartes is charged with saying that animals do not really have any feelings, that they are merely machines.

- A careful reading of his works reveals a more subtle position. While he might have denied them a soul, and self-consciousness, he did not deny them sensation. They communicate their natural instincts and feelings, but they cannot use language as they are not *res cogitans*.

- His use of terms such as automata should not be misconstrued. This meant anything that could move by itself, whether machine, living thing or human.

- Animals might be said to share some level of consciousness and to experience feelings, but are not self-conscious beings in the way that humans are.

- Aware today of the gradation between animals and humans, and the emergence of language from more primitive sounds and communication signals, it would have been helpful for Descartes to have used the Scholastic hierarchy of being system to show that animals had their place in the tree of life and were below, but not that far from, human beings.

Descartes and Feminism

NEW INSIGHTS

Feminist perspectives on the history of philosophy are an original and refreshing method of investigation, raising questions and influences that conventional commentators have avoided. Descartes lived in a patriarchal world and does not directly address the issue of gender, though one of his correspondents (Elizabeth of Bohemia) was female and he latterly worked for Queen Christina of Sweden as her tutor. These two instances alone reveal that he was no male chauvinist, and could see philosophy as a proper subject of study for the female sex.

His methodology of understanding the body as a part of extended reality, and of the indivisibility of the mind led him away from any consideration of the value of male or female physical characteristics. He was not really interested. He wrote about minds and bodies, whether male or female. There is no trace of the masculine being the active agent, and the feminine the passive, as in Aristotelian biology. Here, the male provided the seed which contained the whole embryonic child, and the woman was simply an incubator. In one passage Descartes refutes this, admittedly in the rather primitive-sounding terms of his day:

> it is easy enough to accept that the seminal material of each sex functions as a yeast to that of the other, when the two fluids are mixed together.
> (*The Description of the Human Body*, 1)

For Descartes, men and women's bodies were made of equal stuff, as were their souls. It is possible to find an implicit sexism in his theories, though. There are deeper currents and influences. Feminist study of Descartes focuses on the question of mind and body, and related attitudes towards masculinity and femininity. Issues of power and social influence/dominance underlie these preoccupations, as well as the question of epistemology. A key concern for feminist philosophers is that the cult of reason should not rule supreme; it is one route to knowledge among many. There is also a place for the body, for touch, for emotions and for intuition that cannot always be clearly expressed in words. Their world-view is holistic rather than reductionist.

THE MIND–BODY SPLIT

Leslie Heywood, assistant professor of English Literature at the State University of New York, sees Cartesian influence in the cult of the gym and the struggles of the anorexic. She admits that at first this might seem strange:

> The king of nonbodies, the father of the mind–body split – in a gym? And yet each glistening set of pecs lined up at the mirrors, dumbbells in hand, sweating and pumping away, might be seen as one legacy of Cartesianism. In emancipated bodies, proudly self-starved, anorexics telling themselves their bodies are their kingdoms, wholly separate, disciplined, shaped and contained by their minds, the legacy whispers.
> (Heywood, *When Descartes Met the Fitness Babe*)

Heywood depicts a culture of dominance and violence against women that seeks to shut them off from their bodies. She relates a moving story of her rape when a teenager, describing a personal sense of mental fragmentation as she 'watched' her body carried and penetrated like a lifeless piece of wood. She describes her work with anorexics who seek to withdraw from their bodies into a mental void within. She describes how academia makes women into valuable minds but downgrades their flesh. 'Books were clean. Hard. Masculine.' All of this is the Cartesian legacy. It is linked, in her view, directly with Descartes' First Meditation: 'I will consider myself as having no hands, no eyes, no flesh, no blood, nor any senses …' Why? So that he can think clearly. The mind is a unity, indivisible and thus complete, whole on its own. The body is diverse, made up of many parts. The mind is masculine and the body feminine. As one feminist writer put it: 'A woman's body … stands for all that is inscrutable, unpredictable, and uncertain in life.'

Susan Bordo, professor of philosophy at the University of Kentucky, wrote about anorexia and Cartesian ideology in *The Flight to Objectivity*. With Descartes, there is an opposition between interior and exterior. A wholly interior self is separate from the exterior body. As she says: 'It is only with Descartes that body and mind are *defined* in terms of mutual exclusivity.' The body as machine, as commodity to be sold and controlled, is prey to advertising campaigns and multimillion dollar industries. Sculpting the body that you do not like, with the 'just do it' culture of liposuction and plastic surgery follows on. She concludes: 'Anorexics are "Cartesian", then, in the sense of experiencing (male) mind and (female) body as entirely distinct, with the mind set up as the "dictator" of the flesh.'

VISUALIZATION

Descartes writes about 'clear and distinct ideas' that the mind can perceive and form representations of. He sees with the 'mind's eye', and as he says in *The Meditations*:

> And therefore it seems to me that I can already establish as a general principle that everything which we conceive very clearly and very distinctly is wholly true.

What cannot be so codified, analysed and measured, with mimetic, mental mathematical formulations is outside of the mind's domain and outside of reason. The Cartesian tradition has stressed visual representations over those which are more emotional or involve touch sensations. Feminist philosophy speaks of 'writing the body', valuing the material and the flesh, and exploring bodily metaphors rather than hiding them away. For Luce Irigaray, the director of research in philosophy at the Centre National de la Recherche Scientifique in Paris, women's genitalia are positive images of holes, dark spaces and caves of mystery that house creative potential. She rejects the penis envy of Freud, seeing women as inverting to interiority and the expression of life, rather than lacking something essential. The body speaks of a lack of clearly defined boundaries with its curves and undulations.

There is a sense in which Descartes is unconsciously inconsistent, though. In his opening Meditation, he describes his body and his physical surroundings very carefully – his hands, the fire, the paper and the pen set before him. He admits that this body is a part of him:

> But once more, I cannot perceive without the body, except in the sense that I have thought I perceived various things during sleep, which I recognized upon waking not to have really been perceived …
>
> (Meditation I)

He needs his body in order to think, and when he tries to imagine what his mind would be without it, without food and other physical things, he is certainly not tempted to try to starve himself and see if he can survive without it! It has been pointed out that the *cogito* and the 'I' in *The Meditations* are not always necessarily one and the same. The former is a concept, and the latter is a slippery term. The bare *je* in the French text can mean Descartes the man, the mind and the body, or the thinking self, the cogito. This sense of slippage, which the post-structuralist Derrida describes as **aporia**, (no path) in a text reveals hidden agendas, unguarded ideas and other possible readings than the dominant or the self-conscious one in the mind of the author.

KEYWORD

Aporia: 'no path' in Greek. A term used by post-structuralist or post-modernist interpretation for slippages in a text that reveal a conflict of ideas, often unconsciously.

Ironically, all of Descartes' speculations about his mind and reason are done by a mind in a body, inseparably. They are one man. This sense of aporia can be found in his correspondence with Elizabeth and his insistence upon the radical union of mind and body in the human being. It is disjointed and does not fit the dominant mood of his philosophy. He struggles, lost for words, and ultimately refuses to analyse the nature of the union. It just is. Common sense tells us so. A postmodern, deconstructive reading of Descartes would reveal this slippage and see his elevation of reason and of 'clear and distinct ideas' as not so clear and superior after all.

KEY FACT
DERRIDA AND DECONSTRUCTION

Jacques Derrida has implemented a technique known as 'deconstruction' whereby a text is examined to show the many influences that are at work within it, and the various interpretations that are possible besides the one(s) intentioned by the author(s). He looks for various literary clues that reveal hidden agendas, word links and throwaway statements. Deconstruction reminds us that ideas are partly fashioned by unconscious influences, and we are now ironically self-aware of many of the cultural influences at work in our thinking.

Feminist epistemology needs linking and multidisciplinary concepts that refute and overthrow 'masculine' attempts at dominance. This means that all unified systems are out, as well as the link between true knowledge and the solitary knowing subject. We learn together, in community, and the space between self and the other is vital to this process. We must escape from the slavery of binary opposition, from the dead end of 'either/or'. We must get beyond the number one, and the number two, beyond the solitary and the oppositional. Thus, Descartes did not lay a firm and true foundation for knowledge with his concept of clear and distinct ideas.

KEY FACT
STRUCTURALISTS AND BINARY OPPOSITION

The early to mid-twentieth century movement known as Structuralism began with the Swiss linguist, Ferdinand de Saussure (1857–1913) who developed rules of deep structure for language that he thought could be carried across cultures. This was applied to cultural studies and anthropology by Claude Levi-Strauss (b. 1908) and revolved around the nature of binary opposition, matching and contrasting concepts in pairs such as light/dark, masculine/feminine.

Post-structuralists have attacked this as too rigid. There are some things that just do not fit into contrasting pairs. Language is more elusive. Postmodernism has grown from this linguistic study to question any idea of fixed meanings and foundations of truth.

NATURE AND CULTURE

For Levi-Strauss, nature was 'raw' and culture was 'cooked'. The one had to be tamed and completed by the other. Cartesian ideology seeks to master the environment and the body as a wild thing, imposing masculine order upon it. Cartesian science leads to objectification, separating things from the subject. Feminist interpretation seeks to broaden the analysis, moving out from the objective representations to a more holistic vision involving all the senses and the intuitive, creative faculties. Stop building only world pictures is their message. Feel things, too! Be a part of the whole. Reconnect. It is thought that Descartes and the Rationalists were seeking a minimalist vision, reducing to logical, clear lines of logical perspective rather than a Baroque madness of style and exuberance with its distorted sense of perspective. At least more is included. Less is not always more; sometimes it is just less. This sentiment is captured in the work of the postmodern feminist artist, Barbara Kruger. In her work *We Won't Play Nature to Your Culture*, she has a photograph of an atomic mushroom cloud with the slogan superimposed, 'Your Manias Become Science'. This reflects Nietzsche's claim that any science which harms life cannot be 'true'.

Feminism, with its return to the body, also values a return to nature and a care for the environment. This is not in a simplistic sense, for reason and technology play their part, but complemented and tempered by wider concerns.

WONDER AND SPACE

Irigaray seizes upon some words of Descartes in his *The Passions of the Soul*:

> When the first encounter with some object surprises us, and we judge it to be new or very different from what we formerly knew, or from what we supposed that it ought to be, that causes us to wonder and be surprised; and because that may happen before we know whether in any way whether this object is agreeable to us or is not so, it appears to me that wonder is the first of all the passions ...
>
> (Art. 53)

Irigaray first uses the concept of wonder epistemologically. Wonder is the key to find space to be and to reflect in the presence of something else. It is so easy to be trapped in systems and analysis and in fast-paced techno-living that we have no room to breathe. Wonder provides us with a window to see through to an open space, to relate to the world and the Other. Then we can choose to dwell within it and to transform it. Wonder opens a hole to be whole.

She takes a daring step, contributing to the debate over 'what causes motion' in Descartes' philosophy and that of his contemporaries. It is a fresh, radical œuvre. As she says:

> Wonder is the motivating force behind mobility in all its dimensions.

The living being has a need of wonder in order to move, to be attracted, to be inquisitive and to put oneself in the presence of another. 'Wonder being an action that is both active and passive. The ground or inner secret of genesis, of creation?' Why not include an emotion in the causal principle of motion? We are whole, of a piece, mind and body. We love through the heart, blood and thought, as she puts it.

Irigaray uses the metaphors of accelerating and breaking to suggest a holistic lifestyle. We need rests and stops to reflect and to take time to see what is around us. 'As long as we are embodied, we cannot go beyond a certain rhythm of growth.' The problem is that rationally inspired technology creates a machine that threatens to engulf us with its ever-increasing acceleration.

Resting and breaking helps us to stand in the presence of the other, and men and women are equal but different, strange and wondrous to each other. 'The other never suits us simply. We would in some way have reduced the other to ourselves if he or she suited us completely.' This context recasts questions of the self and the cogito, for *Who art Thou?*, *I am* and *I become* belong to the passion of wonder and to the dynamic of relationship.

DECENTRING THE SELF

Feminist philosophers have been through the school of psychology, trying to come to terms with the inner drives of a person, especially the hidden, repressed, marginalized aspects of ourselves. Some feminist philosophers are also trained and practising analysts such as Irigaray.

> **KEY FACT:**
> **PSYCHOLOGY AND THE SELF**
>
> Sigmund Freud (1856–1939) introduced the role of the *Unconscious*, a deeper part to the Self than we had imagined. His *ego* was the self-conscious self, the cogito, reasoning and controlling the impulses of the chaotic Unconscious. This was comprehended in the light of language as we sought to analyse it and impose order upon it.
>
> One of Freud's disciples, Jacques Lacan (1901–81), worked with a theory of language that led him to hold that the self, the 'I', the cogito, was a social construct. The Unconscious held primal language patterns which helped to form a sense of self as this interacted with society. Much of what we are, our self-identity, he saw as put into us from without. What we are is not always present to our conscious minds. Lacan recast the famous '*cogito, ergo sum*' as follows:
>
> > I think where I am not, therefore I am where I do not think. Is what thinks in my place, then, another I?

The self was only a part of a greater whole, and feminist writers see the self as relating to the Other. A person is this relationship, this mystery. Descartes' rational cogito was too remote and self-contained. The rational part of us is one aspect only.

Feminist philosophers are concerned with social structures and power plays, struggling with the question of what is nature and what is nurture. The feminine has been defined in binary opposition to the masculine, reason is over emotion, and mind over body. Radical feminists sought to overthrow all differentiation in favour of androgyny. Later feminists are more hesitant, seeing women in a process of becoming and self-discovery. Lacan's sense of the self is thus intriguing and appealing for them. They have adapted and developed this, though, seeing the self as innate *and* socially moulded, able to grow and discover itself through relations with others. The self is decentred, a dynamic relationship itself of Unconscious Other and conscious ego, growing and forming in a social world. It is manifold, but it is. It has being.

MADNESS AND REASON

Feminists are wary of the links between hysteria and the feminine condition in Western, patriarchal thought (and all its associations with the womb). The irrational is also seen as feminine with reason as masculine. Reason/irrational stands in a binary opposition, with reason being the primary and thus the preferred term. The French post-structuralist philosopher, Michel Foucault (1926–84), wrote *Madness and Civilization*, a history of attitudes to the insane. He postulated that up until the seventeenth century, the mentally disturbed were out in the open and much more accepted as a part of society. The move to lock them away in asylums began after the elevation of reason. He argued that Descartes had been an inadvertent prime mover in this direction because of his dismissal of the mad in favour of the sane and the rational. Descartes mentions the mad in *The Meditations* when he pulls himself from the brink of the irrational by affirming that he has a body, despite his bout of radical scepticism.

> And how could I deny that these hands and body are mine, unless I am to compare myself with certain lunatics whose brain is so troubled and befogged by the black vapours of the bile that they continually affirm that they are kings while they are paupers, that they are clothed in gold and purple while they are naked; or imagine that their head is made of clay … such men are fools, and I would be no less insane than they if I followed their example.
>
> (Meditation I)

Foucault has been criticized for reading too much into this text. Careful study of *The Meditations* does not deny humanity to the insane. Descartes also pulls himself away from the idea that he is dreaming. This is another form of fantasy and delusion. Dreamers are still human beings, as are the mad. Just because our rational faculties can be 'switched off' for a time does not make us less than human. Whatever the exact interpretation here, Cartesian philosophy (at least after Descartes) did elevate reason and cast the irrational to the fringes, and the feminine did become associated with this for many.

ODE TO WHOLENESS

Feminist critiques of Descartes can be too harsh in claiming him as the render asunder of mind and body. He veered in this direction but turned full circle to cement mind and body in a sublime union. We need our bodies to think and to perceive. He did elevate reason over the emotions, and his doctrine of clear and distinct ideas was truncated thinking. Many things cannot be mentally represented, visualized with the mind's eye or analysed mathematically. These things are not the only 'certain' truth. They are certainly not wholly true, for there is a greater whole. Neither should the self be defined in isolation but in relationship. Existence is societal.

Even the idea of the solitary cogito, radically questioning everything else, can play into feminist hands. Mary Astell wrote *A Serious Proposal for the Ladies* in 1694. A second part to this, written in 1697, distilled the thought of seventeenth-century philosophers such as Descartes and Arnauld. She had used Descartes' scepticism to question all conventions and social taboos. She started with her thinking self and asked why the lot of women could not be different. She advocated forming communities akin to Protestant convents to allow women to live independent lives and to better their education.

Perhaps Descartes' works, like many texts, are capable of being read from different angles. A feminist epistemology would not seek to force them under the dominance of any one interpretation or methodology.

✻ ✻ ✻ SUMMARY ✻ ✻ ✻

- Descartes did not display any overt sexism and treated women as intellectually capable. He did not follow traditional Aristotelian biology, seeing both sexes as co-equal in procreation. He was interested in the common body and mind stuff that both sexes were made of.

- Feminist writers are concerned with the Cartesian legacy regarding the mind–body split. Some trace the obsession with fitness regimes, dieting and the condition of anorexia to a denigration of the body.

- Visualization as the mind's eye of reason is only one valid form of perception. Feminists also stress the value of the other senses, especially touch and the body. There are some things that cannot be visualized or expressed adequately in language.

- Postmodern studies reveal an aporia, a slippage, in Descartes' reasoning in his insistence of a mind–body sublime union and a third primitive notion. Even he did not work with such a rigid binary opposition of mind and body as has been supposed.

- The feminine has been seen as the wild, the hysterical and the mad. Culture and reason have been seen as masculine.

- Wonder allows us to reflect and to cultivate a more holistic, spiritual lifestyle. Reason can produce faster and faster techno-living. It is also a contributing factor in the cause of motion.

- The cogito is only seen as a part of the self now, as the ego and unconscious are as two strangers to each other. The 'self' is something of a social fiction, an association of aspects of mind and language. There is still the thinking, feeling, self-conscious individual at the end of the day, though.

- There is also a paradox that Cartesian methods led to a seventeenth-century woman, Mary Astell, rethinking all that she had been taught and starting again with her own, subjective experience. Paradox and irony, different ways of seeing, are very much a part of the feminist epistemology.

10 Goodbye to Descartes?

Descartes has left abiding questions which have generated discussion in the centuries that have followed:

* Is the mind distinct from the body?
* Can the universe be rationally analysed?

We shall examine each of these in turn.

IS THE MIND DISTINCT FROM THE BODY?

One substance – two substances?

Apart from the religious objections to Descartes' work, various philosophers tackled key elements of his epistemology and sought to correct them. The mind/body problem strained the abilities of many and Descartes careful qualification of radical dualism was often misunderstood or ignored. Even if passing, there were those who sought to declare it illusionary and thus to solve the problem in one blow.

Occasionalist philosophy declared that mental and physical processes were not actually linked – they only seemed to be by a series of coincidences. These are caused by God's intervention so that mental and physical states coincide. The Psychoparellism of Leibnitz (1646–1716) developed this in a more sophisticated manner. He sought a correlation between two completely separate substances (mind and body) that were tuned into each other by God in the beginning, like two clocks set side by side that were originally synchronized.

Spinoza (1632–677) rejected the two substance view entirely and posited a radical and unusual solution. He proposed a monistic solution. His Double Aspect Theory suggests that there is one substance to all reality. Mental and physical actions are two different aspects of this one force. He also called it God.

> ## KEY FACT
> ### THE BRAIN
>
> Early cultures seemed to equate certain feelings or mental states with different bodily organs. In the epics of Homer, for example, the heart is the seat of thought and feelings are in the midriff or bowels. The Greeks had the phrase 'the bowels of compassion'. Some doctors and scholars such as Hippocrates (c. 460–377 BCE) and Galen (129–c. 199 CE), saw the brain as the source of thought and bodily control. Aristotle thought this was the heart, and Plato divided the 'soul' into three parts – the reason, the will and the passions. Reason was linked to the brain, the will was in the chest/lungs, and the passions were in the bowels. Only the rational part of the soul was immortal.
>
> Just prior to Descartes, and contemporary with him, various thinkers began to see the brain as vital to producing thought. This was believed to be in the ventricles, the gaps in the brain, where spiritual forces dwelt. Some, indeed, went further, localizing aspects such as memory, judgement and reason in different ventricles. Descartes himself accepted some of the current ideas, mentioning 'the black vapours of the bile' that are present in the insane, and he speculated that the soul was linked to the brain through the pineal gland.
>
> Gradually, more interest was placed in brain tissue, and functions were mapped out and localized in different parts of the brain such as the cortex. The realization dawned that the cortex housed the higher, voluntary abilities, whereas simple motor functions could be controlled from lower levels of the brain. Nerves, cells, chemicals and electrical discharges were also found to play a part.
>
> The brain is, in fact, a combination of three parts, the forebrain, midbrain and hindbrain. The latter parts are more primitive. The brain has evolved from earlier, basic types, rather as the Windows PC operating system is built upon the older MS-DOS system.
>
> But what *is* the mind?

Brain stuff?

Later researches in biology and psychology have resulted in a great unwillingness to separate mind and brain, recognizing that the mind needs a working brain to exist and to function. Some biologists and neuroscientists are reductionist, seeing consciousness as nothing but the brain working. Physicalists try to equate mental processes with mental states – a thought or idea is a happening in a certain section of the brain. Period.

Behaviourists such as Gilbert Ryle rejected the idea of a 'ghost in the machine' and the actual existence of private, mental events – are only physical behaviours. He spoke of philosophers making 'category mistakes', projecting mental states out into separate, self-existent substances. Hence all metaphysics was a grand illusion, especially Descartes' idea of the soul. It is argued that this ignores our feelings. It actually feels a certain way to be ourselves, the 'I' in my head. Ryle would have replied that such inner, private experience should be seen as dispositions to behave in a certain way. It is one thing saying this of other people, though, and quite another matter when it refers to our own self-reflective life.

KEY FACT
BEHAVIOURISM

Ryle was following Behaviourist principles which were sceptical of allowing any mental states that were not the result of stimuli and responses to physical events. Behaviourism shunned theory and sought statistical data to analyse the behaviour of a person, and downplayed their own intentions. Scientific Behaviourism sought the empirical stimuli and bodily reactions that produced psychological states; methodological Behaviourism applied research and statistics to an individual client's circumstances. The leading Behaviourist thinkers in the early twentieth century were J.B. Watson and B.F. Skinner.

Others take a Functionalist line, seeing the brain as being like a sophisticated computer. Such an attitude can be found in the writings of Dr Stephen Pinker. The mind is summed up as 'the mind is the brain working'.

> The mind is a system of organs of computation, designed by natural selection to solve the kinds of problems our ancestors faced in their foraging way of life, in particular, understanding and outmanoeuvring objects, animals, plants, and other people ... (Pinker, *How the Mind Works*)

Pinker admits that the computation model has its limitations, but it is the best on offer for him. Pinker works for the MIT, the Massachusets Institute of Technology, which has been in the forefront of exploring the possibility of artificial intelligence. Advisers from there worked on the film *2001: A Space Odyssey*. The intelligent computer, HAL, could respond to human language and 'think' for itself. This was their dream in the 1960s, and such possibilities seemed around the corner. Now, people are far more cautious. Pinker, for example, waxes lyrical about robot technology but then says how base and limited this is with the movements achieved by a toddler playing!

Holistic models

Yet others question the computer model as rather limited and artificial. There is the uneasy problem of how mental processes produce physical actions. Computer/mechanical models of the brain treat the mind rather as an *epiphenomenon*, a side effect of the working brain. Computers are not conscious; they process data but are not creative and original. They depend on what you programme into them. A more complex and open model is presented by Dr Susan Greenfield, for example. She is amazed by complexity and keeps a sense of awe as more and more mysteries of the working brain unfold. She appeals to an overall, holistic methodology, rather than experts studying sections of the brain. We must work on the whole brain as a living organism, just as a Beethoven symphony comprises many instruments, players and notes working in harmony. The brain is more than the sum of its parts. It is dynamic. The computational model is rejected, and consciousness must be taken into account as a vital part of the working brain. So, too, we must see the brain as linked with the rest of the body: 'The brain is a part of a body equipped with an immune system, a hormone system and an "automatic" fight-or-flight system for changing the operations of all the vital organs.' This link, this whole, means that we might realize more and more about the impact of mind upon the body, of mental well-being upon physical well-being. Perhaps here we have something of a return to the wisdom of the ancients, recognizing that mental and emotional states affect or are affected by parts of the body.

Greenfield edges towards a definition of the mind as *the personalization of the brain*, and the more advanced and highly developed a brain is, the more its resources, sensory data, memories, feelings and so on form personality. But what, exactly, is consciousness?

Fritjov Capra, too, sees the mind as a process rather than a self-contained, static thing, and the brain as the structure that allows this process to operate. The whole body is a unity, a network that acts together, and the nervous system, the immune system and the endocrine system form a single, cognitive network, so much so, that the brain and the body cannot really be separated. A key phrase for Capra is *interdependence*. He appeals to ancient concepts of the soul or spirit as 'the breath of life', pointing out that these words are linked with breath – *atman* in Sanskrit, *pneuma* in Greek, *ruach* in Hebrew. Thus, the mind, the rational aspect, was a part of a greater whole, the life process.

KEY FACT
DO RELIGIONS HAVE TO TEACH THAT THERE IS A SOUL?

Hebrew thought did not countenance a separable, immortal soul. The 'soul' was a part of the whole person. Jewish faith developed a belief in some kind of *resurrection* as a result. We had to be 'raised' in a new body after death. There might not be a part of us that survives without the re-creating power of God. Christianity adopted this, but the developing theology of the new faith was worked out in Hellenistic culture, with a strong belief in the immortality of the soul. The Church tended to teach a two-stage doctrine of post-mortem existence – the survival of the detached, immortal soul, and the clothing of this with a new body at the general resurrection of the dead at the end of time.

Cognition for Capra is not just an internal representation of an outer world, but a bringing forth of a world, whereby our ideas and feelings make actions that change things. We are not just information processing machines, but creators, utilizing the crucial role of language in human evolution We are a social mind as well as a biological or personal one. We are a process, and perhaps many things in interaction produce the 'self' and we cannot pin down a fixed self within this, over and above the flow.

Modern dualism

There are many who do hold to a mind–body dualism, and a strong belief in an immortal soul. Besides religious dogma, there are the near death experiences (NDEs) which people relate. These are fascinating and widespread, and it is impossible to verify them scientifically. They are certainly very real to the experient. This form of dualism would admit that there are close and vital links between the brain and the body, but one should not make the mistaken assumption that we can simply reduce thought and feelings to these material things. The hypothesis is advanced that the mind might use the brain rather as television signals need a television set to be tuned in to and to be watchable. In all fairness, this is still an open question. Even Descartes, with all his talk of dualism and innate powers of reason, could not avoid the problems and the profundity of the actual interaction between mind and body. It was a puzzle to him, ultimately, that he never adequately explained.

KEY FACT
NEAR DEATH EXPERIENCES

These describe the conditions experienced by a patient who nearly dies, usually during surgery, and returns to life by being resuscitated. There is a common pattern of feeling that they are floating above their bodies, and a tunnel opens up with bright light at one end. In the light, they might see friends, gardens, or Jesus/and angel/a Being of Light.

These were first reported by psychiatrist Raymond Moody in Virginia in 1965, after he had heard George Ritchie tell his story. He went on to collect some 150 cases. These were followed by Kenneth Ring, a social psychologist from Connecticut, publishing his methodical research in 1980. Then, a paediatrician from Seattle, Dr Melvin Morse, collected many stories from children. In the UK, a neurophysicist, Dr Peter Fenwick, collected more than 300 examples. People seem to have these more frequently than was realized, and they did not say anything for fear of ridicule in a materialistic society. Convinced materialists like Susan Blackmore, a psychiatrist from the University of the West of England in Bristol, offer other explanations. She tries to explain NDEs by the chaos sparked off in the cerebral cortex of the brain as the brain is dying. A mixture of endorphins and oxygen starvation might account for the tunnels, the sense of being out of the body and the bright lights. Those who have experienced NDEs are not impressed, as the experience feels so real and illuminating. It is an open question.

What is Consciousness?

There is no way of avoiding the mystery and the value of consciousness. It feels a certain way to be 'me' and to be self-aware, and the human *qualia* cannot be simplistically reduced to neurons firing with electricity and chemical processes. But what, exactly, is consciousness? Consciousness might be said to be made up of many parts or levels:

- Consciousness as wakefulness can be rooted in the action of certain parts of the brain, such as the reticular formation, the *pons* the *raphe nuclei* and the *locus coeruleus*. Destruction of the former leads to coma, for example.

- Consciousness as sensory experience can be rooted in visual processing areas of the brain, and if these are damaged, then we might not see or be aware of certain things.

- Consciousness as working memory uses different parts of the left and right hemispheres of the brain, in the frontal cortex of the brain.

Consciousness is thus many things working together, and cannot be localized in any one part of the brain (even Descartes tried to link soul and body through the pineal gland). Many parts of the brain work together to form our conscious experience, and there is the irreducible mystery of what makes the 'me' in my head. Self-awareness is more than wakefulness, sensory experience or working on a task in hand. Psychology has also delved deeper than the conscious, rational ego into the hidden depths of the unconscious. The 'self' has depths and aspects that we are not always aware of. Let Susan Greenfield have the final word, here:

> Consciousness brings the mind alive; it is the ultimate puzzle to the neuroscientist. It is your most private place. This ultimate puzzle, the subjective experience of consciousness, is perhaps a good place for any purely scientific survey, namely one of objective facts, to cease.
>
> (Greenfield, *The Human Brain: A Guided Tour*)

The mystery of 'me' means that we still cannot quite saying 'Goodbye' to Descartes.

CAN THE UNIVERSE BE RATIONALLY EXAMINED?

A mathematical universe?

Descartes was convinced that mathematics revealed the underlying principles and regular structures of 'extended reality'. Allowing for occasional errors, he was happy to rely on this form of knowledge as a way of really seeing the external world. What was out there corresponded to what his mind deduced in theorems and abstract patterns and numbers. His belief in God secured this further beyond all doubt.

The ancient Greeks had explored mathematics and saw the world as governed by these geometric rules. Pythagoras (c. 550–500 BCE) was a philosopher-mystic who thought that numbers were divine and should be worshipped! Mathematics predated and pre-existed the human mind. Plato followed this, seeing mathematics as the real foundation of reality. In a way, mathematics is universal, with fractal patterns in nature from sub-atomic levels to crystals and clouds. Fibonacci numbers (1, 2, 3, 5, 8, 13 etc) are found in some flowers like sunflowers.

Discoverers or inventors?

But how far do we discover and how far do we invent mathematics? Our calculations might be limited to our brains, as though we are designed to see things in a certain way, rather as a certain model of computer can handle only certain data, but a more advanced one can produce a very different analysis because it can process more and more data. If our brains are wired in a certain way, then we will only perceive reality in that way. An alien intelligence might see the universe in a different manner. Formalists argue that mathematics is thus merely a human construct, an elaborate game of rules like chess that can produce beautiful theorems but has little relation to reality. Platonic mathematicians disagree and see regularities across the universe that can be predicted mathematically, such as black holes.

Richard Dawkins, for example, while he admits that our brains run a limited software programme, can still embark on a fascinating adventure of virtual reality:

> We can take the virtual reality software in our heads and emancipate it from the tyranny of simulating only utilitarian reality. We can imagine worlds that might be, as well as those that are. We can simulate possible futures as well as ancestral pasts. With the aid of external memories and symbol-manipulating artefacts – paper and pens, abacuses and computers – we are in a position to construct a working model of the universe and run it in our heads.
>
> We can get outside the universe. I mean in the sense of putting a model of the universe inside our skulls ... (Dawkins, *Unweaving the Rainbow*)

But it is still only a model, amazing but limited.

What of 'clear and distinct ideas'?

Descartes mathematical reductionism of extended reality found something of a new lease of life in the researches of Noam Chomsky (b. 1928). He worked on the stucture of language at Harvard University. He broke sentences down into component parts and charted complicated structural 'syntax trees' for what seemed to be simple sentences, such as 'the large black dog licks the tabby kitten'. This became:

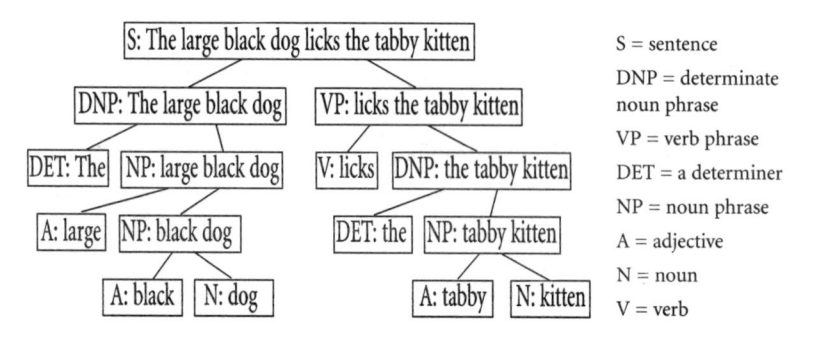

```
S: The large black dog licks the tabby kitten
   ├── DNP: The large black dog
   │      ├── DET: The
   │      └── NP: large black dog
   │             ├── A: large
   │             └── NP: black dog
   │                    ├── A: black
   │                    └── N: dog
   └── VP: licks the tabby kitten
          ├── V: licks
          └── DNP: the tabby kitten
                 ├── DET: the
                 └── NP: tabby kitten
                        ├── A: tabby
                        └── N: kitten
```

S = sentence
DNP = determinate noun phrase
VP = verb phrase
DET = a determiner
NP = noun phrase
A = adjective
N = noun
V = verb

He argued that all human language could be analysed and broken down into a 'hard-wired Universal Grammar'. Chomsky was involved with the MTI and was an early pioneer of theories of artificial intelligence. If we understood the code of human language, then we could replicate this in computers. We have not yet succeeded.

Critics point out that we have to see language in action, in context, and not as an abstract concept. It is used in communication by human beings who use bodily gestures, silences, facial expressions and have their own feelings. Communication cannot be reduced to mathematical logic. It just is not *human*.

Descartes' contemporary, Blaise Pascal, once remarked that mathematics was limited:

> Mathematicians wish to treat matters of perception mathematically, and make themselves ridiculous ... the mind ... does it tacitly, naturally and without technical rules.
>
> (Pascal, *Pensées*)

Mathematical knowledge might be very useful and a powerful tool, but it is one-dimensional. Might Descartes' difficulty in linking mind/body lie in the rigidity of his categories? The philosopher Stephen Toulmin has spoken of the 'omega trajectory' of recent thought. Following the shape of the Greek letter Omega (Ω) he postulates that the ancients had a more holistic, spiritual view of reality, whereas the Enlightenment heritage was to climb away from this to a more logical and mathematical model. This is like climbing up from the base of the Ω. In recent years, we have been moving right round the curve to the bottom again. We have a more mysterious, holistic vision whereby we cannot separate mind and body, or person, from context or observer from experiment. As Toulmin concludes:

> Descartes' *foundational* ambitions are discredited, taking philosophy back [to that of an earlier era].
>
> (S. Toulmin, *Cosmopolis*)

Round the Curve

The new physics, or quantum mechanics, has opened up the world to be a stranger, more random place, though. The Uncertainty Principle asserts that we cannot trace the position and the speed of a particle at one and the same time with any degree of accuracy. There is a whole picture that eludes us. Think, again, of how modern physicists observe that light behaves in some ways like particles and in other ways like wave patterns. This stretches our minds to the limits of rationality. (How far could this model be deemed to be a 'clear and distinct' idea by Descartes?) This brings us back to the issue of how limited our brains are. We are also much more aware of the blurring of the divide between subject and object in our perceptions, and our experiments and measurements are effected. What we see and understand is limited to our abilities.

Kant's spectacles

Kant rejected the notion that we could have innate and immediate awareness of truth and reality whether by 'clear and distinct' ideas or any other means. Everything, but everything, was filtered through our senses and our awareness/consciousness. How we saw the world was conditioned and never pure, even if mathematics came closer to a purer form. He spoke of the *noumenal* and the *phenomenal* worlds. The former is reality as it is in itself, whereas the latter is how we perceive things to be. There is a correlation, a correspondence, otherwise we would not be able to live in the world and make sense of anything, but we have a limited vision. It as though we see everything through a pair of spectacles through which we filter information. Only God can see the noumenal world as it is.

He also spoke of absence and presence. The world as it is in itself is not able to be directly present to us. Reality is tantalizingly absent and yet present through interpretation. Our self-consciousness is not present to ourselves as Descartes thought. How we think things, how we understand ourselves and our feelings are also a matter of interpretative absence. All is interpretation.

The postmodern condition

Postmodern philosophers have taken Kant to sceptical lengths. All knowledge is seen as time and culture conditioned; there is no pure form of knowing. There is a suspicion of metanarratives, or grand narratives. Jean Francois Lyotard (1924–99) wrote of this impossibility, for all our grand narratives are partial distortions, limited and somewhat local. Any age has set ideas and outlooks that influence and prejudice thought. Lyotard also suggested that we do not know what advances human evolution might bring, and what expanded intelligence might perceive. We can never say we know it all. All we are capable of is a series of local and limited truths.

> Let us wage a war on totality; let us be witnesses to the unpresentable; let us activate the differences and save the honor of the name. (Lyotard, *The Postmodern Condition*)

This shakes the foundations of Descartes' philosophy and casts doubt upon the certainty of the conscious mind and inner, deducible truths. Postmodernists also attack binary oppositions as the foundations of truth. Binary oppositions such as truth/falsehood, light/dark, mind/body are not the only way of seeing the world. Jacques Derrida has pointed out that not everything fits so neatly into these patterns. There are things or states which he calls 'undecidable', as an android in science fiction is not really alive or dead. We cannot always answer 'Yes' or 'No'. Sometimes it is 'Both/and'. The mystery of mind/body is one such undecidable.

God cannot so easily be appealed to now so as to guarantee truth. Postmodern thinkers vary in their faith, atheism or agnosticism, but even if we have faith, it must be in a post-Kantian sense whereby God only guarantees the world as it is in itself, and not as we see it. We cannot step outside of ourselves, our perceptions or our language.

We are left with partial glimpses and useful ideas, though, and there is the vast, unpresentable mystery of existence, what postmodernists call 'the Gift', in which we live and move and have our being. Discourse and reasoning have not completely broken down; we are just humbler.

IN MEMORIAM

Descartes tried to establish a dispassionate system that sought a cool rationality that could study phenomena in isolation of observer or context. This ambition has been thrown into question in the twentieth and early twenty-first centuries from so many directions. There is a recognition that we need to value, but to nonetheless move beyond logic. Various studies have shown that the emotions play a part in a balanced mind that reasons. Brain-damaged persons might still be able to make logical deductions and perform rational tasks, but with their emotional side impaired, they actually display alarmingly irrational behaviour. Examples of this were presented in Antonio Damasio's book, *Descartes' Error*. Damasio is a neurologist who could show that a person who could perform highly on IQ tests could not live their lives in any sort of balanced or safe manner. Psychologists have always declared that repressed emotions cause psychic malfunction; so, too, do impaired emotions. In politics, the totalitarian regime that brooks no ridicule or satire but forces an empty conformism is anti-human. So, too, is any attempt to sterilize life by seeking a coolly rational and detached laboratory approach to our problems. We are *human beings*.

Descartes was a pioneer of the scientific method, though, and despite its limitations, this has been a radical paradigm shift in the history of thought. There is no denying its many advances and inventions, but it has also produced global pollution and atomic bombs. We need *soul*, too. He gave us that aplenty, and there is no exorcizing *that* ghost. We might question it, reject some concepts of it, refuse a radical duality, but it pops up time and again in the mystery of consciousness, as the self of whom we are aware in all its irreducible mystery. And despite all that we know about mechanics, physical forces, laws and electric/chemical impulses in the brain, are we really any closer to understanding how our thoughts can move things?

There is that which is undecidable, which cannot be categorized as fixedly 'either/or'. Reason breaks down and mystery leads us on.

* * *SUMMARY* * *

- The mind/body problem has exercised thinkers down the ages. Occasionalists saw the links as God's direct intervention, Spinoza as two aspects of one substance. Twentieth-century Behaviourists scorned the idea of a 'ghost in the machine' and saw mind as a function of the physical brain.

- Computational models see the mind as the brain working, as a side effect of the brain. More holistic models stress the interrelationship of many aspects and brain areas that produce the wonderful mystery of consciousness that no one is able to explain. There are still versions of full-blown dualism with the soul using the brain as signals use a television set.

- Mathematics can be very useful and go a long way to understanding the universe, but it is human and limited. What would alien mathematics be like? Our brains are wired to understand only so much. The models we construct are like a virtual reality programme.

- Chomsky tried to find a mathematical basis for language, hoping that thinking, talking computers would be on the horizon. However, communication implies emotions and human *qualia* that go beyond logic.

- There is an attempt to climb around the Ω to return to more expressive, intuitive ideas today. There is also a tendency to suspect grand narratives with the critique of postmodernism and any unified theories. The concept of undecidability that goes beyond binary opposition is useful. Mind–body relationships then can be seen in a different light.

GLOSSARY

Anaclastic Parallel lines intersect when passing through a fluid as a result of a change in the angles of reflected light.

Aporia 'No path' in Greek. A term used by post-structuralist or postmodernist interpretation for slippages in a text that reveal a conflict of ideas, often unconsciously.

Automaton Literally an object that is self-moving. This might or might not imply consciousness. It need not mean a 'mere machine'.

Causa secundum esse A cause of being. Once an act is completed, its effects cease, unless they are continuously repeated.

Causa secundum fieri A cause of becoming. The effects of the causal agent continue.

Causal adequacy Causes are as real as their effects.

Cogito, ergo sum 'I think (or I am thinking) therefore I am.'

Epistemology The nature of knowledge, its sources and methods of learning.

Extended reality That which is measurable and quantifiable. It has length, breadth and height, weight and motion.

Final cause The Schoolmen thought that an object was made with a purpose in mind by God, which was its final cause. So, fire burned, warmed and moved upwards because of its in-built, inner propensity to do so.

Hierarchy of being There is a chain of being, whereby some things are more real than others, the infinite more real than the finite and so on.

Index of Forbidden Books A list of prohibited literature whose teachings were said to contradict the Church's faith and morals. This was instituted in 1557 and lasted until 1917! Special permission had to be sought to read anything on this list.

Libertines Atheistic freethinkers who rejected Scholasticism and the teachings of the Church.

Metaphysics The realm of truth beyond the natural world. The question of Meaning, of Being and the foundations of truth.

Occasionalist Someone who believes that God directly causes motion, and secondary effects from impact of bodies are mere 'occasions', by-products of God's will-in-action. Some thinkers saw God as continually re-creating objects from moment to moment in different points in space.

Ockham's razor A principle elucidated by William of Ockham (*c.* 1287–1347) whereby unnecessary facts or arguments are stripped away to get at the basic idea.

Ontological argument The claim that if an idea of perfection can enter the human mind, then to be perfect, it must also exist in reality. Thus, if no greater Being than God can be imagined, there must be a God.

Paradigm shift A shift in perception and the models we use to understand reality. Thomas Kuhn (b. 1922) coined the term, poking fun at a naive and progressive view of science. Our knowledge did not always gradually grow like a slow escalator, but it came in flashes of inspiration, in leaps and as a result of new discoveries that render previous paradigms obsolete. Sometimes there is suspicion and conflict as the old order gives way. Descartes and the early Rationalists found exactly this from the Church and the Schoolmen.

Quadrivium The academic study of arithmetic, geometry, music and astronomy as the main four sciences of the early seventeenth century.

Rationalist Someone who believes that true knowledge comes from reason, and is more reliable than that apprehended by the senses through contact and observation.

Reductio ad absurdum A reduction to the absurd, taking an argument to its most extreme and absurd level.

Reductionist Analysing the external world as reducible to the sum of its parts, to basic, physical properties. Today the term tends to imply that a thinker denies the existence of an immaterial, immortal soul or the spiritual realm. This was not true for Descartes and many seventeenth-century reductionists. A distinction was drawn between the mental/spiritual and the physical.

Scholasticism The ideas of the Greek philosophers, especially Aristotle, which were the basis of medieval intellectual life prior to the time of Descartes and were interpreted by the Church.

Theist A believer in God, the Supreme Being.

Unified theory A 'Theory of Everything' which seeks to find underlying forces or equations behind different physical forces and laws.

FURTHER READING

General Introductions to Descartes' life and thought:

* *Introducing Descartes* by Dave Robinson and Chris Garratt (Icon Books, 1999)
* *Descartes* by John Cottingham (Phoenix Press, 1997)
* *Descartes: A Very Short Introduction* by Tom Sorell (Oxford University Press, 2000)

Biographies covering his life and the development of his philosophy in context:

* *Descartes* by Bernard Williams (Penguin Books, 1978)
* *Descartes – An Intellectual Biography* by Stephen Gaukroger (Oxford University Press, 1997)

Articles and essays on various aspects of Descartes:

* *Descartes* edited by John Cottingham (Oxford University Press, 1998)
* *Descartes Embodied* by Daniel Garber (Cambridge University Press, 2001)
* *Goodbye Descartes: The End of Logic and the Search for a New Cosmology of Mind* by Keith J.Devlin (Barbour Publishing, 1998)
* *Descartes' Error* by Antonio R. Damasio (Papermac, 1996)
* *Feminist Interpretations of René Descartes* edited by Susan Bordo (Penn State Press, 1999)
* *The Cambridge Companion to Descartes* edited by John Cottingham (Cambridge University Press, 1992)

Philosophical writings by Descartes:

* *Philosophical Essays and Correspondence* edited by Roger Ariew (Hackett Publishing Company, 2000)

- *Selected Philosophical Writings of Descartes* edited by John Cottingham, Dugald Murdoch and Robert Stoothoff (Cambridge University Press, 1998)
- *Key Philosophical Writings: Descartes* (Wordsworth Editions Ltd, 1997)
- *A Discourse on Method, Meditations and Principles: René Descartes* translated by John Veitch, edited by Tom Sorell (Everyman, 1994)
- *Discourse on Method and Related Writings* translated by Desmond M. Clarke (Penguin Books, 1999)

INDEX

anaclastic 14
aporia 64
Aquinas, Thomas 1, 44
Aristotle 1–2, 9
Arnauld, Antoine 39, 47, 53
Astell, Mary 70–1

Bacon, Sir Francis 13
Beeckman, Isaac 7
Behaviourism 74
binary opposition 65, 83
Bordo, Susan 63
Bourdin, Pierre 30

Capra, Fritjov 76–7
Cartesian Circle 34
causal adequacy 35
Chomsky, Noam 80–1
Christina, Queen of Sweden 11–12, 61
clear and distinct ideas 20–1, 33, 80–1
cogito 27, 29, 46, 58
contact theory 42
Copernicus, Nicholas 3
corpuscles 17
cosmological argument 37
consciousness 78–9

Damascio, Antonio 84

Elizabeth of Bohemia 49–52, 61

empiricism 22–3
Enlightenment 2, 42
epistemology 4
extended reality 20, 46

final cause 21
Foucault, Michel 69

Galileo 3, 15
God 9, 16, 27–8, 33–45, 51–3, 84
Greenfield, Susan 75–6

Heywood, Leslie 62
hierachy of being 36

Ignatius of Loyola 25
Irigaray, Luce 63, 66–7

Kant, Immanuel 37, 82

Lacan, Jacques 68
La Flèche 7, 9, 13
Leibnitz, Gottfried Wilhelm 72
libertines 9
Lyotard, Jean Francois 83

Mersenne, Marin 9–10
metaphysics 1
moral argument 37

near death experiences 77–8
Newton, Sir Isaac 17

Occasionalism 40–1
Ontological argument 28, 36–7

Paley, William 42
Pascal, Blaise 38, 81
pietists 39
Pinker, Stephen 74
Plato 79
post-modernism 64, 83–4
primitive notion 49
Pythagoras 79

quadrivium 14

Rationalist 23
reductionist 19–20
Renaissance 2
res cogitans 20
Rosicrucians 15
Ryle, Gilbert 47, 74

sceptics 30–1
Scholastics (Schoolmen) 1, 2, 13
Sorbonne 9, 30
Spinoza, Benedict 72

teleological argument 37
Toumlin, Stephen 81–2

Ultimate Reality 37
unified theory 15

qualia 54